Grade 5

Frank Schaffer Publications®

Editor: Linda Triemstra
Interior Designer: Lori Kibbey

Frank Schaffer Publications®

Send all inquiries to:
Frank Schaffer Publications
3195 Wilson Drive NW
Grand Rapids, Michigan 49534

Read 4 Today—grade 5

ISBN: 0-7682-3215-5

2 3 4 5 6 7 8 9 10 PAT 10 09 08 07 06 05

Read 4 Today

Table of Contents

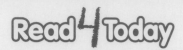

Introduction

Read 4 Today supplies predictable, patterned review and practice materials for students. Four questions a day for four days a week provide students with the opportunity to hone their skills. A separate assessment is included for the fifth day of each week. On odd-numbered weeks, students will work on decoding or word strategies, vocabulary, fluency, and comprehension; on even-numbered weeks, the activities focus on book titles and previewing, with students answering questions before, during, and after reading. This book covers a forty-week period, and each grade level includes some curricula from the previous and the following grade levels.

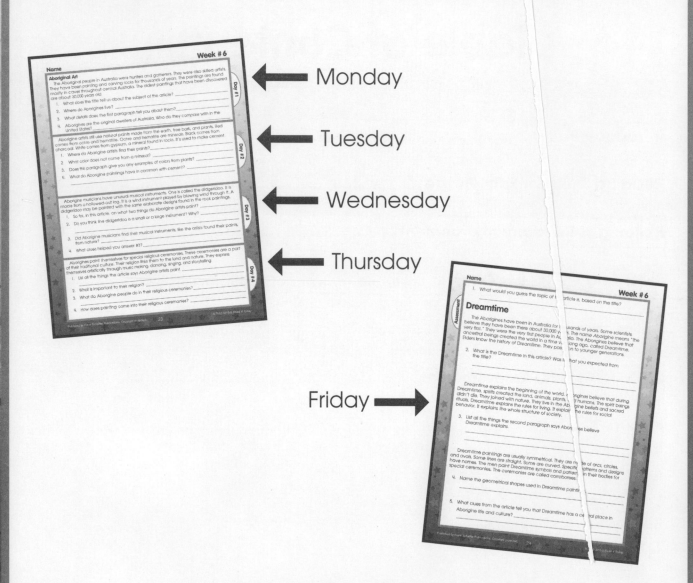

Monday

Tuesday

Wednesday

Thursday

Friday

Skills and concepts are reinforced throughout the book, and it incorporates the style and syntax of standardized tests. The answer key reproduces each page, both daily practices and assessments, for ease in grading.

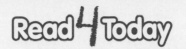

Reading Skills and Standards for Fifth Grade

Fluency

- ꙮ read text aloud with appropriate pacing, intonation, and expression
- ꙮ comprehend what is read as it is read (short time from reading to comprehension)
- ꙮ repeated practice in reading text aloud from student's "independent" level (approximately 1 in 20 words difficult for the reader)

Vocabulary

- ꙮ use word origins to find meaning of unknown words
- ꙮ use context to find meaning of unknown words
- ꙮ identify Greek and Latin roots, suffixes, and prefixes to analyze the meaning of complex words
- ꙮ determine part of speech, pronunciation, and meaning of words using a dictionary

Comprehension

- ꙮ establish purpose for reading
- ꙮ identify main idea and supporting details
- ꙮ make predictions based on evidence in text (inferencing)
- ꙮ distinguish between fact and opinion
- ꙮ identify and analyze organizational structures in text (cause and effect, compare and contrast, chronological order)
- ꙮ summarize information
- ꙮ answer literal, inferential, and evaluative questions
- ꙮ identify the genre of a literary text
- ꙮ identify story elements (characters, setting, plot, problem, solution)
- ꙮ understand figurative language and its function in text (simile, metaphor, hyperbole, personification)
- ꙮ self-monitor comprehension

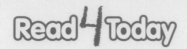

Building a Reading Environment

The reading environment is essential to fostering successful readers. When building a positive reading environment, think of students' physical, emotional, and cognitive needs.

Physical Environment

- Make the physical reading environment inviting and comfortable. Create a reading corner with comfortable chairs, floor pillows, a rug, enticing lighting, and so on.
- Give students access to a variety of text by providing books, magazines, newspapers, and Internet access. Read signs, ads, posters, menus, pamphlets, labels, boxes, and more!
- Provide regularly scheduled independent reading time in class. Encourage students to read at home. They can read to a younger sibling, or read anything of interest, such as comic books, children's and sports magazines, chapter books, and so on.
- Set a positive example. Make sure students see you reading along with them!

Emotional Environment

- Learn about students' reading habits, preferences, strengths, and weaknesses, and then provide books that address these issues.
- Help students create connections with text. Facilitate connections by activating prior knowledge, examining personal meaning, and respecting personal reflections.
- Give students the opportunity to choose titles to read. This gives them a sense of ownership, helping to engage them in the text and sustain interest.
- Create a safe environment for exploring and trying new things. Foster a feeling of mutual respect for reading abilities and preferences.
- Require that students read at an appropriate reading level. Text in any content area, including leisure reading, should not be too easy or too difficult.
- Get all students to participate in reading, no matter what their reading level. Try not to alienate slower readers. Give them time to finish before moving on or asking questions.
- Be enthusiastic about reading! Talk about books you love, and share your reading experiences and habits. Your attitudes about reading are contagious!

Cognitive Environment

- No matter the grade level, read aloud to students every day. Reading aloud not only provides a good example but also lets students practice their listening skills.
- Help students build their vocabularies to make reading more successful. Create word walls, personal word lists, mini-dictionaries, and graphic organizers.
- Read for different purposes. Reading a novel requires different skills than reading an instructions manual. Teach students the strategies needed to comprehend these texts.
- Encourage students to talk about what and how they read. Use journal writing, literature circles, class discussions, conferences, conversations, workshops, seminars, and more.
- Writing and reading are inherently linked. Students can examine their own writing through reading and examine their reading skills by writing. Whenever possible, facilitate the link between reading and writing.

Skills and Concepts   Odd-numbered weeks

Skills and Concepts   Odd-numbered weeks

week 25—page 61

beginning sounds
middle sounds
ending sounds
prefixes and suffixes
adjectives
synonyms
details
context clues
cause and effect
paraphrase
reading out loud
compare and contrast

week 27—page 65

vowel sounds
ending sounds
rhyming
synonyms
homophones
details
context clues
making inferences

week 29—page 69

middle sounds
syllables
synonyms
antonyms
title clues
author's purpose
details
reading out loud

week 31—page 73

beginning sounds
silent letters
consonant blends
synonyms
homographs
author's feelings
context clues
fact and opinion

week 33—page 77

vowel sounds
silent letters
compound words
synonyms
point of view
genre
rhyme scheme
context clues
author's purpose

week 35—page 81

consonant sounds
syllables
synonyms
roots
suffixes
reading out loud
point of view
context clues

week 37—page 85

consonant sounds
roots
suffixes
syllables
rhyming
synonyms
antonyms
author's purpose
main idea
context clues

week 39—page 89

silent letters
consonant sounds
consonant pairs
synonyms
paraphrase
main idea
details
cause and effect
making inferences

0-7682-3215-5 *Read 4 Today*

Skills and Concepts   Even-numbered weeks

week 2—page 15

title clues
supporting details
subject
compare and contrast
conflict and resolution
reading in the content areas:
    math

week 4—page 19

genre
title clues
character
details
setting
context clues
paraphrase
cause and effect
moral of the story

week 6—page 23

title clues
details
compare and contrast
context clues

week 8—page 27

title clues
author's feelings
details
context clues
compare and contrast
reading in the content areas:
    math

week 10—page 31

title clues
characters
compare and contrast
making predictions
details
context clues

week 12—page 35

prefixes
title clues
main idea
paraphrase
supporting details
compare and contrast

week 14—page 39

title clues
genre
character
paraphrase
idioms
cause and effect
context clues

week 16—page 43

title clues
context clues
cause and effect
making inferences
details

week 18—page 47

title clues
genre
synonyms
details
main idea
making inferences
details
idioms

week 20—page 51

title clues
details
context clues
cause and effect

week 22—page 55

title clues
fact and opinion
context clues
conflict and resolution
making a chart

week 24—page 59

title clues
synonyms
supporting details
character
compare and contrast
making predictions

Published by Frank Schaffer Publications. Copyright protected.

0-7682-3215-5 *Read 4 Today*

Skills and Concepts   Even-numbered weeks

week 26—page 63

title clues
setting
details
reading in the content areas:
    math
context clues

week 28—page 67

title clues
fact and opinion
author's feelings
details
reading in the content areas:
    math

week 30—page 71

synonyms
title clues
compare and contrast
making a chart
context clues
reading in the content areas:
    math

week 32—page 75

title clues
supporting details
setting
context clues
character
alternate title

week 34—page 79

title clues
fact and opinion
context clues
cause and effect
character
making predictions

week 36—page 83

title clues
synonyms
topic sentences
sequencing
context clues

week 38—page 87

title clues
context clues
metaphors
similes
making inferences
compare and contrast
making a chart

week 40—page 91

title clues
fact and opinion
details
author's purpose

Published by Frank Schaffer Publications. Copyright protected.

0-7682-3215-5 *Read 4 Today*

Scope and Sequence

Skill	1	2	3	4	5	6	7	8	9	10	11	12	13	14	15	16	17	18	19	20
beginning sounds:	•				•		•	•												
middle sounds:			•		•	•	•		•	•			•		•		•			
ending sounds:			•				•				•		•							
consonant pairs/blends:					•		•		•		•		•				•		•	
vowel pairs:					•				•		•		•		•			•	•	
compound words:	•		•		•		•		•		•		•		•		•	•	•	
synonyms:	•		•	•			•						•							
antonyms:	•		•		•		•		•				•		•					
roots:	•								•						•					
prefixes:	•											•			•					
suffixes:							•				•									
syllables:	•								•				•							
silent letters:							•													
homographs:																				
homophones:													•		•					
main idea:			•				•		•	•		•		•	•			•	•	•
cause and effect:	•	•		•	•	•	•	•	•	•		•		•	•	•	•	•	•	•
compare and contrast:										•			•							
context clues:	•	•		•	•	•	•	•	•	•		•		•	•	•	•	•		•
title clues:		•		•						•		•		•	•			•		•
character:													•				•			
conflict and resolution:																				
genre:											•								•	
details:	•	•	•	•	•	•	•	•	•	•	•	•	•	•	•	•	•	•		•
making predictions:																				
contractions:				•										•						
author's feelings:											•									
author's intention/purpose:				•										•				•	•	•
fact and opinion:																				
setting:					•												•			
rhyming:		•						•												
reading in the content area:												•		•	•		•	•	•	•
sequencing:				•																
idioms:	•										•						•			
paraphrase:				•						•		•	•					•		
moral of the story:				•																
topic sentences:					•															
onomatopoeia:									•											
making inferences:								•	•	•		•		•	•		•	•	•	
different endings:													•							
reading out loud:				•						•							•			
making a chart:		•		•	•	•											•			
other:	•	•	•	•			•	•	•	•	•	•	•	•	•	•	•	•	•	•

T = Weekly Test   • Indicates Skill or Concept Included and/or Tested

Scope and Sequence

	21	T	22	T	23	T	24	T	25	T	26	T	27	T	28	T	29	T	30	T	31	T	32	T	33	T	34	T	35	T	36	T	37	T	38	T	39	T	40	T
beginning sounds:	•																•				•																			
middle sounds:	•		•		•				•		•										•																			
ending sounds:	•								•												•																			
consonant pairs/blends:													•								•								•						•		•			
vowel pairs:					•		•																						•								•			
compound words:	•		•		•		•		•				•				•				•		•		•		•						•				•			
synonyms:	•				•				•														•				•													
antonyms:					•												•								•															
roots:																																					•				
prefixes:			•		•				•				•		•						•												•				•			
suffixes:					•																•																•		•		
syllables:					•																•																•				
silent letters:	•		•		•				•								•								•						•		•						•		
homographs:																					•				•		•										•				
homophones:																					•																•				
main idea:					•																																•				
cause and effect:	•										•				•												•										•		•		
compare and contrast:								•																	•																
context clues:	•		•				•		•		•		•		•		•		•				•		•		•		•		•		•		•		•		•		
title clues:			•				•												•		•		•		•		•								•		•		•		
character:			•																				•																		
conflict and resolution:									•		•																														
genre:	•				•		•		•				•		•		•		•		•		•		•		•		•		•		•		•		•		•	•
details:	•						•																•		•				•				•				•		•		
making predictions:	•						•																		•				•												
contractions:	•																				•																				
author's feelings:	•																				•																				
author's intention/purpose:																					•				•						•										
fact and opinion:			•																																						
setting:													•										•																		
rhyming:															•												•														
reading in the content area:																																									
sequencing:																					•								•						•						
idioms:																																			•						
paraphrase:			•																														•								
moral of the story:																																									
topic sentences:																																									
onomatopoeia:	•																																								
making inferences:					•		•										•						•						•								•		•		
different endings:																															•				•		•		•		
reading out loud:			•						•																•		•				•										
making a chart:			•																																						
other:	•		•		•		•		•		•		•		•		•		•		•		•		•		•		•		•		•		•		•		•	•

T = Weekly Test   • Indicates Skill or Concept Included and/or Tested

0-7682-3215-5 *Read 4 Today*

Diego came down with the flu on Monday night. His doctor told him to stay home from school for the rest of the week. She told him he could do schoolwork on Thursday, but not to overdo it.

1. "Over" is a prefix that means "too much" or "more than usual." So what does **over** + **do** mean?_____

2. Which phrase matches the doctor's advice to Diego: "Do schoolwork but take it easy" or "Be sure to do all your schoolwork"? Circle it.

3. How many days was Diego home not doing schoolwork? _____

4. Is having the flu an excuse to ignore your schoolwork? Why or why not?
_____

Day #1

Joe and Gabby needed information for their report on theropods. It was hard to find resources on this dinosaur. They decided not to get another topic. They would leave no stone unturned while looking for information.

1. Circle all the words with three syllables.

2. What are *resources*?_____

3. Are theropods common dinosaurs to study? What detail helped you answer that question? _____

4. Underline the correct meaning of "leave no stone unturned." a) They will turn over every stone they see to look for theropod fossils. b) They will look for information everywhere.

Day #2

Rebecca didn't finish her math homework last night. She played on the computer instead. She asked her mother to tell her teacher that she had been sick. Her mother told her that she would have to face the music herself.

1. Circle the compound word.

2. What is one word that says what Rebecca asked her mother to do?_____

3. Did Rebecca make a good choice? Why or why not? _____

4. What does "face the music herself" mean?
_____

Day #3

One morning at school, you see your friend looking dreamy-eyed. On her paper she has drawn hearts and flowers.

1. Does the beginning sound of *school* sound like the beginning sound of **skate** or **shoot**?_____

2. What is the opposite of *dreamy-eyed*? _____

3. Do you want to ask your friend about the reason for her behavior? Why or why not?_____

4. What do you think is happening with your friend? _____

Day #4

Assessment

The Test

Billy knew that he was in trouble...big trouble. Ms. Keaton, his teacher, had seen him cheating on his test. She hadn't said anything yet, but Billy knew that she'd seen him peek at the little piece of paper hidden in his hand. He chewed on his pencil for a minute and thought. He had to get rid of that paper. But how?

"Billy, if you are finished with your test, would you please come up here?" Billy nodded. His heart was pounding so hard that he couldn't speak. He bent down to tie one of his shoes. Could he stuff the paper in his shoe? No, Ms. Keaton was watching him...waiting for him.

Billy glanced out the window. It was a beautiful spring day. But he wouldn't be going out for recess. He'd probably never get to go out for recess again. He swallowed hard. If only he had studied last night, instead of watching that TV show! Then, on the bus this morning, he decided to write down a few science facts on a piece of paper and hide it in the palm of his hand. It had been a crazy idea, and now he was going to pay for it.

Billy walked up slowly to Ms. Keaton's desk. In a flash, he had an idea! As he stood by her desk, he could open his hand so that the paper fell into her wastebasket. Later, he could try to get it back again. It was a great idea!

Ms. Keaton smiled at Billy. "Since you finished first," she said, "I thought you might like to help me set up our science experiment."

Billy was stunned. What luck! Ms. Keaton hadn't seen his little piece of paper. Now all he had to do was get it into the wastebasket. As he nodded, he opened his hand. The paper fluttered down. A sudden breeze from the open window pushed it a it fell. It floated down to Ms. Keaton's feet.

Billy, you dropped this," said Ms. Keaton. She picked it up. Then she looked at it more closely. "What exactly is this?" she asked, looking worried.

1. List two words that rhyme with *loose*. _____

2. Find two words in paragraph 6 that could be synonyms._____

3. Mark each of these parts of the story with an **E** for an important event or **D** for a story detail.

   _____   a.   Billy watches TV instead of studying.
   _____   b.   Ms. Keaton calls Billy up to her desk.
   _____   c.   Billy ties one of his shoes.
   _____   d.   Billy's heart pounds.
   _____   e.   Ms. Keaton picks up the paper.
   _____   f.   Billy thinks about recess.

4. Did Billy think it was a good idea to cheat on his test at the beginning of the story? Did he change his mind by the end?_____

5. What does "pay for it" mean? _____

_____

The Underground Railroad

The Underground Railroad wasn't a railroad at all. It was a group of people who helped slaves escape to freedom. Those in charge of the escape effort were often called "conductors." The people escaping were known as "passengers." And the places where the escaping slaves stopped for help were often called "stations."

1. What does the title tell you the subject of the selection might be?

   _____

2. Does the opening sentence **support** or **contradict** your guess?_____

3. What is the subject of this selection?_____

4. What does the opening paragraph tell us about who is involved? _____

Day #1

Like a train ride, the Underground Railroad moved people along. Those who escaped often followed routes that had been laid out by others before them. However, unlike a train ride, some routes went underground through dirt tunnels without any sort of tracks.

1. What comparison does this paragraph make? _____

   _____

2. How is the subject like the thing it's compared with? _____

3. How is the subject unlike the thing it's compared with?_____

   _____

4. How does this paragraph make you feel? _____

Day #2

Escaping slaves had to be certain that they could find their way. They needed food and water to make the journey. Conductors helped guide them and provide supplies. One of the most famous Underground Railroad conductors was Harriet Tubman. She had escaped slavery herself. Another famous conductor was Levi Coffin.

1. What part of the subject does this paragraph focus on?_____

2. What was their job? _____

3. Name two famous conductors. _____

4. What details did you find out about any of the conductors?_____

   _____

Day #3

Experts disagree about how well the Underground Railroad was organized. Still, it is believed that the system helped thousands of slaves reach freedom between 1830 and 1865.

1. What problem did the Underground Railroad try to solve?_____

   _____

2. What new details did you learn? _____

3. How many years did the Underground Railroad operate? _____

4. Imagine traveling the Underground Railroad. Did you imagine yourself as the slave or the conductor? _____

Day #4

1. A quilt is like a sandwich: fabric as the "bread" and cotton filling as the "peanut butter." What practical reason would a person have to make a quilt?

   a. to stay warm   b. to use as kindling   c. to eat

Quilts Reflect a Culture

Many African women knew how to sew when they came to America as slaves. They were skillful seamstresses. Sometimes these seamstresses sold for as much as $1,000 on the slavery block.

2. What was the effect of a slave's ability to sew? _____

   _____

   _____

Some slaves made quilts for their owners. They used the scraps from those quilts to make quilts for their own families. Those quilts often told the story of their families. These quilts were called story quilts.

3. Did quilts have only practical purposes for the slaves who made them? What clues from the paragraph help you answer that question?_____

   _____

   _____

A slave named Elizabeth Keckley supported 17 people by sewing. In 1855, she made enough money to buy freedom for herself and her son. That freedom cost her $1,200. She moved to Washington, D.C. There she sewed for President Lincoln's wife. She made a quilt that probably used scraps from Mrs. Lincoln's gowns.

4. How do you think Elizabeth Keckley got the scraps from Mrs. Lincoln's gowns to make her quilt?

   _____

   _____

   _____

5. What do you think is the most surprising or interesting fact in the last paragraph? _____

   _____

   _____

A tarantula is a big, hairy spider. You might see one in a pet shop that carries unusual pets. In the United States, tarantulas live in the West, where it is hot and dry. During the day, tarantulas sleep in holes and other dark places.

1. What word above has a *t* that is pronounced like **ch**?_____

2. Give antonyms for *big, hairy*._____

3. If you visit a pet shop that carries unusual pets, you might see

   a. a cat.   b. a canary.   c. a tarantula.

4. What might happen if you stuck your hand in a dark hole in Arizona?_____

   _____

Day #1

Tarantulas catch their food mostly by jumping on it and biting it. Smaller tarantulas eat insects. Larger ones eat mice and lizards. A tarantula's poison can kill the animals it hunts, but its poison cannot kill a human.

1. Circle the word that has an ending sound like the middle *t* in *tarantula*.

2. What is another word for "the animals it hunts"?

   a. prey   b. toast   c. pray

3. What information in this paragraph might make you feel better about meeting up with a tarantula?_____

4. What kills the animals a tarantula hunts?_____

Day #2

If you are bitten, you soon know that a tarantula bite hurts only about as much as a bee sting. Its bite helps the spider protect itself. The shy tarantula bites humans only if it feels threatened and cannot get away.

1. Is the *i* in *bite* pronounced the same as the *i* in *bitten*? _____

2. What is another word the author could have used instead of *shy*? _____

3. What might happen to someone bitten by a tarantula?_____

4. Poking or touching a tarantula might make it

   a. run away.   b. bite you.   c. run until it catches you.

Day #3

A tarantula has another way to protect itself. It can rub its hind legs together, which causes its stiff leg hairs to fly up in the air. Each tiny hair can make a hurtful skin or eye wound.

1. Circle all the words that have a short **i** sound.

2. Which meaning of *wound* is correct here: **wrapped around** or **injury**?_____

3. What details does the writer use to describe tarantula hairs? _____

4. If you looked closely at a tarantula rubbing its hind legs together, what might happen?

   _____

Day #4

Venus Flytrap

Kayla got a Venus flytrap for her birthday. She put it with her other plants on her windowsill. She watered all of her plants each day.

After a week, all of her plants looked fine except for the Venus flytrap. She decided that she needed more information on this plant, so she went to the library and found a book about the Venus flytrap.

She was surprised to find out that this plant was carnivorous, or meat-eating. No wonder it was not doing well! The book said that the Venus flytrap is a popular house plant. Each set of leaves stays open until an insect or piece of meat lands on the inside of the leaf. The two leaves close quickly, trapping the bait inside. After a leaf digests the meat, it dies. A new leaf grows to take the place of the dead leaf.

Now Kayla knew how to take care of her Venus flytrap.

1. Complete this sentence with a homophone of *week*: After a week the Venus

    flytrap was _____ .

2. What does the word *carnivorous* mean?_____

    _____

3. What clues can you get from the compound word in the name of the *Venus*

    flytrap about what it might eat?_____

    _____

    _____

4. Why did Kayla need to go to the library? _____

    _____

    _____

5. What do you think Kayla will do next?

    _____

    _____

    _____

The Fox and the Crow

A crow found a piece of cheese on the ground. It quickly swooped down to pick up the food and perched on a limb to enjoy the tasty treat. A fox wandered by and saw this.

1. This is one of Aesop's fables. What is a fable?
   a. a funny story   b. a true story   c. a story that teaches a lesson

2. What does the title tell us about the characters?_____

3. Do we meet both characters in the first paragraph? _____

4. What was the first thing the crow did after grabbing the cheese?_____

   _____

"Good afternoon, Crow," the fox called out politely. "How lovely you look today! I bet your voice is just as beautiful so that you sing the sweetest melodies of all the birds in the forest."

1. Why do you think the fox said nice things to the crow? _____

2. Have you ever heard a crow before? If so, do you think It makes a beautiful sound?
   _____

3. What about the crow did the fox actually compliment?_____

4. During what time of day does this fable take place? _____

The crow began to feel very vain as she listened to the fox. She puffed up her feathers, lifted her beak into the air, and opened her mouth to show the fox her musical voice. Just as she did this, the cheese fell out of her mouth and tumbled to the ground. The fox grabbed the cheese and hungrily devoured it.

1. Why did the crow drop the cheese? _____

2. Do you think the fox meant those compliments? _____

3. What was the first thing the fox did after grabbing the cheese?_____

4. What clues tell you that the fox was probably hungrier than the crow?_____

   _____

The fox smiled slyly. As he walked away, he called back to the speechless crow, "I will give you some words of wisdom, little Crow. Do not trust those who praise you with many compliments."

1. Restate the fox's message in your own words._____

2. What other message works?
   a. Always share your cheese.   b. Always compliment others.   c. Never listen to a fox.

3. Has anyone ever complimented you to get you to do something he or she wanted? If so, did it work? _____

4. Have you ever complimented someone to get what you wanted? If so, did it work?
   _____

Assessment

1. By reading the title, do you think this is one of Aesop's fables? _____

The Oak and the Reeds

A mighty oak grew along a riverbank. Its trunk was thick, and its branches reached upward into the sky. It towered proudly above a patch of reeds that grew below it along the edge of the water.

2. What type of objects are the two characters in this fable?_____

_____

On most days, a breeze blew across the river. The leaves of the mighty oak danced, but its branches held firmly in place. The oak laughed at the reeds because the wind was not so kind to them. The reeds trembled and shook as they struggled to stand up straight. But the reeds did not mind the laughter of the oak; after all, the tree was so much bigger and stronger.

Then one day, a terrible hurricane approached the river. Its violent winds pulled up the roots of the mighty oak and tossed it to the ground. When the storm was over, the great tree lay in the patch of reeds.

3. How is the oak tree different from the reeds?

_____

_____

The oak spoke sadly, "The strong winds were able to pick me up and throw me to the ground like a stick. Yet you reeds were able to stay rooted even though you are much smaller. How could this be?"

One reed spoke. "We may be small, but we know how to bend, whether the wind blows gently or violently. You, mighty oak, were too proud and did not know how to bend."

4. What caused the oak tree to fall?

_____

_____

5. What is the lesson of this fable?

   a. It can be better to be flexible than to be strong.

   b. It's okay to laugh at those smaller than you.

   c. Stay out of the way of a hurricane.

Green plants are like factories. Plant factories make two kinds of food: one is sugar, and the other is starch. Almost all fruits and vegetables you eat contain some form of sugar or starch. Fruits like apples, oranges, cherries, pears, and even lemons contain sugar; vegetables like potatoes, corn, and beans contain starch.

1. Circle words with a soft **g** sound and put a line through words with a hard **g** sound.

2. What is a factory? _____

3. With what does the author compare green plants? _____

4. What two kinds of food do plant factories make? _____

_____

Green plants are made up of cells just as you are. A cell is the smallest structural unit of a living organism, whether it is a plant or an animal. Because they are so small, cells can be seen only through a microscope. Inside the cells are chloroplasts, which contain chlorophyll and carotene. They manufacture the sugar and starch; therefore, they are the machines of the plant factory.

1. List the words that begin with the same starting sound as **clean**. _____

_____

2. What is a microscope? _____

3. What is compared with the machines of a factory? _____

4. Can you see cells with the naked eye? _____

There are two kinds of doors in plant factories. One kind is called stomata. Stomata are tiny holes in the leaves that allow air to move in and out. Plants use carbon dioxide and then release oxygen back into the air. Roots are the second kind of door. Water travels into the root hairs of the plant.

1. Put a circle around words with *oo* that sound like **boots**. Put a line through words with *oo* that sound like **floor**.

2. What are stomata? _____

3. Which is a better title for this paragraph: **Stomata in the Leaves** or **Doors of the Factory**? _____

4. What are the two kinds of doors in plant factories? _____

Plants use storerooms to store their food. Carrot plants store their food in roots, while maple trees store their food in trunks. Lettuce plants store their food in leaves, peas store their food in seeds, and peach trees store their food in the fruit.

1. Find and circle a compound word.

2. What word could you use instead of *store* as it is used in this paragraph?

_____

3. What is the topic sentence of this paragraph? _____

_____

4. Match the plants to their storerooms.

carrot	fruit
lettuce	root
peas	trunk
peach tree	seeds
maple tree	leaves

Assessment

Have you ever watched a coach during a ball game? The coach tells players where to go and what to do as things are happening in the game. Your brain is like your coach. Information from your five senses—touch, smell, hearing, taste, sight—races to your brain. Your brain sorts out the information and lets your body know what to do.

Your brain has three main parts, the medulla, cerebrum, and cerebellum. Perhaps you have heard someone talk about "gray matter" while discussing intelligence. This refers to the cerebrum. The cerebrum is large, and its outside layer is gray and looks wrinkled. The cerebrum, the cerebral cortex, springs to work when you are doing something that requires a good deal of thought. If you are taking a test, talking to a friend, or reading directions to put together a new bicycle, your cerebrum is busy.

As you try to keep your balance on your bicycle, it is your cerebellum that is called to work. The cerebellum is in control of balance and coordination. It is much smaller than the cerebrum.

The medulla is your brain stem. It is the lowest part of your brain. The medulla controls breathing and heart rate.

The next time you put together a bicycle, take a bike ride, and gasp for breath after riding up a hill, you will know that all the parts of your brain have been very busy.

1. List the words that have to do with the brain that start with a soft **c** sound.

    _____

2. What is the cerebral cortex?

    _____

    _____

3. To what does the idiom *gray matter* refer?

    _____

    _____

4. With what does this article compare your brain? Why?

    _____

    _____

5. Make a chart that details which part of the brain controls which function and gives an example of that function.

Aboriginal Art

The Aboriginal people in Australia were hunters and gatherers. They were also skilled artists. They have been painting and carving rocks for thousands of years. The paintings are found mostly in caves throughout central Australia. The oldest paintings that have been discovered are about 30,000 years old.

1. What does the title tell us about the subject of this article? _____

2. Where do Aborigines live? _____

3. What details does the first paragraph tell you about them? _____

4. Aborigines are the original dwellers of Australia. Who do they compare with in the United States? _____

Day #1

Aborigine artists still use natural paints made from the earth, tree bark, and plants. Red comes from ochre and hematite. Ochre and hematite are minerals. Black comes from charcoal. White comes from gypsum, a mineral found in rocks. It's used to make cement.

1. Where do Aborigine artists find their paints? _____

2. What color does not come from a mineral? _____

3. Does this paragraph give you any examples of colors from plants? _____

4. What do Aborigine paintings have in common with cement? _____
   _____

Day #2

Aborigine musicians have unusual musical instruments. One is called the didgeridoo. It is made from a hollowed-out log. It is a wind instrument played by blowing wind through it. A didgeridoo may be painted with the same elaborate designs found in the rock paintings.

1. So far, in this article, on what two things do Aborigine artists paint? _____

2. Do you think the didgeridoo is a small or a large instrument? Why? _____
   _____

3. Did Aborigine musicians find their musical instruments, like the artists found their paints, from nature? _____

4. What clues helped you answer #3? _____

Day #3

Aborigines paint themselves for special religious ceremonies. These ceremonies are a part of their traditional culture. Their religion links them to the land and nature. They express themselves artistically through music making, dancing, singing, and storytelling.

1. List all the things the article says Aborigine artists paint. _____
   _____

2. What is important to their religion? _____

3. What do Aborigine people do in their religious ceremonies? _____
   _____

4. How does painting come into their religious ceremonies? _____

Day #4

Assessment

1. What would you guess the topic of this article is, based on the title?

    _____

Dreamtime

The Aborigines have been in Australia for thousands of years. Some scientists believe they have been there about 30,000 years. The name *Aborigine* means "the very first." They were the very first people in Australia. The Aborigines believe that ancestral beings created the world in a time very long ago, called Dreamtime. Elders know the history of Dreamtime. They pass it on to younger generations.

2. What is the Dreamtime in this article? Was it what you expected from the title?

    _____

    _____

Dreamtime explains the beginning of the world. Aborigines believe that during Dreamtime, spirits created the land, animals, plants, and humans. The spirit beings didn't die. They joined with nature. They live in the Aborigine beliefs and sacred rituals. Dreamtime explains the rules for living. It explains the rules for social behavior. It explains the whole structure of society.

3. List all the things the second paragraph says Aborigines believe Dreamtime explains.

    _____

    _____

Dreamtime paintings are usually symmetrical. They are made of arcs, circles, and ovals. Some lines are straight. Some are curved. Specific patterns and designs have names. The men paint Dreamtime symbols and patterns on their bodies for special ceremonies. The ceremonies are called corroborees.

4. Name the geometrical shapes used in Dreamtime paintings. _____

    _____

5. What clues from the article tell you that Dreamtime has a central place in
    Aborigine life and culture? _____

    _____

Teddy just about fell out of his seat. Mrs. Beeker, his science teacher, announced that during the following week the class would go to the Colgate Nature Preserve to examine pond life! That meant he'd be free to splash away in the water in search of his beloved leopard frogs!

1. Which letter in *leopard* is silent? _____

2. When is *the following week*?

   a. that week   b. the next week   c. two weeks from then

3. What effect did the setting of his class trip have on Teddy?_____

4. What do you think a leopard frog looks like? _____

Day #1

The next week, the class boarded a waiting bus and rode off to the rural setting of Dilly Pond. Students scooped and trowled for larvae, crustaceans, and small fish. They observed birds, mammals, and amphibians in the wetlands. And Teddy mucked around in the rushes among the creatures of frog heaven.

1. Which word ends with the same ending as *oceans*? _____

2. Does *rural* mean **in the city** or **in the country**? _____

3. List all the items the kids interacted with in the wetlands. _____

   _____

4. What does the author mean by *frog heaven*? _____

   _____

Day #2

That was thirty years ago. But Teddy still remembers. As he prepares the science laboratory for his students, his mind returns to the pond that glorious fall day so many years ago. It was the day that he first knew what he wanted to do with his life. It was one of the best days he could remember.

1. Does the *ou* in *glorious* sound like the *ou* in **out** or **serious**?_____

2. What other word (two syllables or more) could you use instead of *glorious*?

   _____

3. What is Teddy's job today? _____

4. What effect did the field trip to Dilly's Pond have on Teddy's life? _____

   _____

Day #3

With a whimper, Daisy hung her head and looked at me beseechingly.

1. *Beseechingly* has two suffixes. What are they? _____

2. When Daisy looks beseechingly, is she **begging** or **angry**? _____

3. Does Daisy sound happy? What clues helped you answer that question?

   _____

4. What do you think Daisy is? _____

Day #4

Assessment

Aquarium Competition

Jake opened the lid of his aquarium. Most of the fish quickly swam to the top. They knew it was time for dinner. Jake paused before sprinkling the food across the water. He noticed that one little fish stayed away from the others. Its fins were looking ragged. Jake wondered whether the fish might be sick.

Jake tapped the can, and the food fell out. He saw one big fish rush to the top and gobble up most of the food. This same fish nipped at the fins of the smaller fish whenever it tried to grab a bite.

"I see why its fins are ragged," thought Jake. "That little fish isn't sick at all. The bigger fish is just picking on it."

Jake got out a smaller fish bowl. He poured some tank water into the bowl, scooped the ragged fish out of the aquarium with a net, and gently put it in the small bowl.

"There you go, little guy!" said Jake. "I'll give you lots of food and some time to grow. When you get big and strong, I'll put you back in the aquarium again. Then you will be able to compete with that bully fish!"

1. Find a word that begins with a soft **g** sound. _____

2. What does it mean to be a bully? _____
    _____

3. What is the effect of the big fish gobbling up all the food?
    _____
    _____

4. In this story, what does *compete* mean?
    a. to get to the top of the tank faster
    b. to be a bigger bully
    c. to grow bigger than the others

5. Try to predict what will happen to the little, ragged fish now.
    _____
    _____
    _____

Those Wacky Australian Animals

Australia's animals are unique. They include marsupials and monotremes. Both are mammals. Marsupials carry their babies in pouches. Monotremes give birth to their young by laying eggs, but they produce milk to feed their babies.

1. What clues does the title give us about the subject of this article? _____
_____

2. What word in the title tells us the author has a sense of humor about the article? _____

3. What is distinctive about monotremes? _____

4. What is distinctive about marsupials? _____

Day #1

The Tasmanian devil is a ferocious marsupial that lives on the island of Tasmania. These animals have black fur and very sharp teeth. They eat other mammals, birds, and reptiles.

1. What kind of animal is the Tasmanian devil? _____

2. What clues does the paragraph give you that is deserves the name *devil*?
_____

3. How did the *Tasmanian* part of its name come about? _____

4. Is the Tasmanian devil a carnivore? _____

Day #2

The duck-billed platypus is one of two animals that hatches its young from eggs. It has soft fur, a snout, webbed feet and claws, and a flat tail like a beaver's tail. They live near rivers and creeks, where they eat crawfish, worms, and small fish.

1. What kind of animal is the duck-billed platypus? _____

2. What animal is compared with the duck-billed platypus in the paragraph? _____

3. Look at the list of characteristics of the duck-billed platypus. List other animals that share one characteristic. You may want to make a chart.

4. What do you think of the duck-billed platypus's looks? _____
_____

Day #3

Kangaroos are herbivores. Baby kangaroos, called joeys, live in their mother's pouch for 5 to 6 months. Kangaroos can hop at about 40 miles per hour (about 64.3 kph). They have strong hind legs for leaping about 30 to 40 feet (about 9 to 12 m).

1. What does an herbivore eat?
   a. meat   b. plants   c. metal

2. What kind of animal is a kangaroo? _____

3. How does a kangaroo get around? _____

4. Is the author right? Are some Australian animals wacky? _____
_____

Day #4

Assessment

1. This title gives a lot of information. What does it tell us the author will do in this article?

_____

Australia and the United States: Alike or Different?

How are Australia and the United States alike? How are they different? Australia is in the Southern Hemisphere. The United States is in the Northern Hemisphere. Australia's summer months are December through February, which are the United States' winter months. Summer months in the U.S. are June through August, which are Australia's winter months. In the Northern Hemisphere, hurricanes and tornadoes spin in a clockwise direction. In the Southern Hemisphere, they spin in a counterclockwise direction.

2. Suppose that your birthday is December 11. Compare the activities you could do at your birthday party if you lived in Australia and if you lived in the United States.

_____

_____

_____

Australians drive on the left side of the road, while people in the United States drive on the right side of the road. Australia's population is about 19 million. That's about the same as the total of the six most populated cities in the United States. Australia has kangaroos, anteaters, emus, and koalas, but in the United States you'll find those animals only in zoos.

3. Do more people live in Australia or in the United States?_____

The official head of Australia's government is the queen of England. In the United States, it is the president. Australians elect people to a legislature, and a prime minister is the functional head of government. There are three major political parties there, but only two in the U.S. An Australian law says that people who are able to vote must vote. If not, they can be fined. There's no law like that in the United States.

4. Put the following topics in the order they appear in the article: population, politics, climate, wildlife, customs. _____

_____

5. What do you think is the most interesting difference between Australia and the United States? _____

28

"Quiet down, students, and please go to your desks," Mr. Chan said to the class. He waited for everyone to get settled. "Now, please take out your writing journals. Today, we will be learning about inferencing."

"Is that like conferencing?" Daphne asked eagerly. The students often held conferences to discuss their stories, and Daphne had just finished a good story.

1. The word *conferencing* will help you with pronouncing *inferencing*. What do the two words share in common? _____

2. What are conferences?_____

3. Does Daphne like conferencing?_____

4. What clues helped you answer #3?_____

"No," replied Mr. Chan. "But that's a good guess. In fact, that's what inferencing is—it is making an educated guess based on what you already know. Then, you add to it any new information you receive. Daphne saw that we were using our journals and inferred that we would be doing something that involved writing. Good inferencing, Daphne!"

1. Which letter is silent in *guess*? _____

2. *Prior knowledge* is a phrase that could be used instead of what phrase in this paragraph? _____

3. What does Mr. Chan compare inferencing with?_____

4. What is the difference between a **guess** and an **educated guess**?
   _____

Just then, a loud, clanging noise rang through the room. The students put down their materials and lined up at the door. They walked single file out to the playground. All the other students soon joined them. This had happened many times before, so the students knew what to do.

1. Circle a compound word in this paragraph.

2. What word in this paragraph sounds like what it means? _____

3. What was the loud noise?_____

4. What clues from the paragraph helped you answer #3? What information you already know helped you answer #3? _____
   _____

After waiting a long time on the playground, the restless students began to wonder. They usually did not have to wait this long before returning to their classrooms. All at once, a red truck with a ladder on top drove up to the school.

1. *Ai* and *ay* sometimes sound the same. List the words in this paragraph where *ai* and *ay* sound the same. _____

2. What are the root and the suffix in *restless*? What does *restless* mean? _____
   _____

3. Were the students **frightened** or **bored**?_____

4. Do you think this is a fire drill or a real fire? How do you know?_____
   _____

Assessment

An Inferencing Incident

The students began talking anxiously. Some men and women raced around to the side of the building carrying a water hose.

The students became nervous as they saw the men and women direct the hose to where a puff of smoke was coming out of a window near the school's cafeteria. Mr. Chan went to talk with the principal as the students watched in concern.

"Don't worry," Mr. Chan reassured them a moment later. "Everyone is safe. The situation will be taken care of shortly. But I'm going to make an inference. I infer that we may be eating lunch in our classroom today instead of in the cafeteria!"

1. What sound does the *x* in *anxiously* make?_____

2. What other word could you use instead of *anxiously*? _____

3. What word tells you how much smoke was coming out? Does it tell you there was a lot of smoke or just a little? _____

_____

4. Was this a fire drill or a real fire? Compare this answer with the one you gave to this question earlier this week.

_____

_____

5. Do you think Mr. Chan's inference is correct? Explain. _____

_____

_____

The Dark and Stormy Night

"I love reading Fright Night books," said Devon, as he put down his book. "This one is about a girl who got locked in a basement. Another scary-looking girl appears. Frances, the girl in the basement, can see right through her, and..."

1. What does the title tell you about what kind of story this might be? _____
   _____

2. To which character(s) are we introduced? _____

3. Does this character like scary stories? _____

4. Do you like scary stories? Why or why not? _____

Day #1

"Too scary for me," said Tomas. "I don't want to hear anymore."

"It's not that scary," laughed Talia.

"I like the feeling of a good scare," said Linnette.

1. Which new character(s) are introduced? _____

2. Compare each student's reaction to scary stories (don't forget about Devon).
   _____

3. Predict what might happen to Tomas if Devon keeps telling the scary story.

4. Why do you think people like to read scary stories? _____

Day #2

"Then you wouldn't mind going to my new house," grinned Talia. "We just bought the Perkins place at the edge of town."

"That's crazy!" said Devon. "Spooky old man Perkins died in that house years ago. Nobody has been in it for years. What's wrong with your old house?"

1. What was wrong with the house Talia's family bought? _____

2. Would you move to a scary house? Why or why not? _____

3. Does Talia sound frightened of her new house? _____

4. What clues from the paragraph helped you answer #3? _____
   _____

Day #3

"Nothing," said Talia, "but this one is bigger and has a huge yard for our pets."

"Okay, I'll go," each friend agreed in turn. They couldn't let Talia go alone, even if it was to be her new home. "To be continued..."

1. What do you know about Talia's character from the story? _____

2. Are Talia's friends **supportive** or **uncaring**? How do you know? _____
   _____

3. Did the author mention a dark and stormy night? _____

4. What does "to be continued..." mean? _____

Day #4

Assessment

1   What does the title tell you about what this story will be about?

_____

The Dark and Stormy Night: Part Two

The friends met and rode their bikes to the old Perkins house after dinner. It didn't look so bad in the twilight. Suddenly, it began to rain, then thunder and lightning crashed through the sky, which quickly turned dark.

"Oh, no!" said Devon. "It's a dark and stormy night. Something awful is going to happen. And I just thought of something else. It's Friday the thirteenth!"

2. Is there any new information in the above paragraphs that make sense of the title? If so, what?_____

The group turned their bikes around and began to leave. Just then a tree fell to the ground and blocked their exit. "We'll have to go in the house," said Talia. They got off their bikes and followed her as if going to their doom. When Talia opened the door, it creaked. Suddenly they heard footsteps walking towards them. The friends looked for a place to hide, but it was too dark. "Ouch!" said Linnette as she bumped into a wall. Everyone began to scream.

"What's going on?" said a voice.

3. What details make this paragraph scary?_____

_____

The lights went on. The house was warm and cozy and filled with furniture. The storm seemed far away. The old Perkins place had changed from the neighborhood haunted house into the perfect place for Talia's family.

"Welcome to our new home," said Talia's dad. "Talia told us she was bringing you all. I think maybe she didn't tell you we were settled here already. Have some hot chocolate and cookies. It's a dark and stormy night out there. Call your parents and ask them if you can stay a while. After all, tomorrow is Saturday."

The group looked around the room. Talia was lucky. "Come on, I'll give you a tour," Talia said proudly. "This place is full of nooks and crannies and secret places, thanks to Mr. Perkins. We can pick one and sit to tell ghost stories."

"I think I've had enough scary stuff for tonight," said Linnette.

"This is more fun than a Fright Night book," said Devon. And everyone agreed.

4. What negative did Talia's dad turn into a positive?_____

5. Write a different ending for the story. _____

_____

32

Imagine an island surrounded by deep, blue seas; covered with lush, green plants; and decorated with mounds of brilliantly colored flowers. A cool Pacific breeze carries the fragrance of the flowers and the ocean water to you as you relax on a warm, sandy beach. Add to that the sounds of plunging waterfalls and tropical birds. These are the sights and sounds of a paradise called Hawaii.

1. Is the ending sound of *paradise* like the ending sound of **wise** or **ice**? _____

2. What is a *paradise*? _____

3. What is the purpose of this paragraph? _____

4. Which sense described in the paragraph is missing from the last sentence? _____

The beautiful islands of Hawaii make up the youngest member of the United States. Hawaii joined the union on August 21, 1959. It is located in the middle of the Pacific Ocean, far from the mainland of the continental U.S. It is also the southernmost state, reaching as far south as central Mexico.

1. What is the suffix in the word *southernmost*? _____

2. What is a synonym for *middle*? _____

3. Which words does the author use to describe the physical position of Hawaii?

   _____

4. What geographical comparison does the author make? _____

Hawaii consists of a chain of 122 volcanic islands, eight of which are considered its main islands. All of the people of Hawaii live on seven of the eight islands. Honolulu, Hawaii's capital, is located on Oahu. Oahu is home to over three-fourths of Hawaii's population.

1. Rewrite *three-fourths* as a fraction. _____

2. What does *volcanic* mean? _____

3. What fraction of the islands do people live on? _____

4. Which island do most Hawaiians live on? _____

Hawaii, nicknamed the Aloha State, offers unique traditions and friendly people. *Aloha* means *love* in the Hawaiian language. Islanders often greet tourists with a garland of strung flowers called a lei. Visitors also enjoy delicious food, ukulele music, and hula dancing at popular feasts called luaus. Many of these customs are traditions of the Pacific Islanders, called Polynesians, who were the original settlers of Hawaii.

1. Find a compound word in this paragraph. _____

2. What word in the paragraph means *love*? _____

3. What are traditions? _____

4. Which customs does this paragraph mention? _____

Hawaii

Assessment

Today, Hawaii is a melting pot of many nationalities and racial groups. Hawaii's population includes people of Polynesian, Chinese, Filipino, and Japanese descent. All of these peoples have contributed to the diverse lifestyle of the state.

Since Hawaii is situated in the middle of the Pacific Ocean, it provides a strategic location for U.S. military presence. The money spent on salaries for military personnel and civilian employees by the U.S. government provides the largest source of income in the state. The second largest source of income is agriculture, which includes huge crops of sugar cane and pineapple. Tourism is yet another large income provider as hundreds of thousands of tourists visit each year.

Whether a native Hawaiian or a visitor from anywhere around the globe, most would agree that Hawaii is a slice of heaven on earth.

1. List the words that have two vowel pairs in a row. What are the pairs?

    _____

    _____

2. What does *melting pot* mean in this paragraph?

    a. Hawaiians put people in a big hot pot.

    b. It's too hot in Hawaii to cook with pots.

    c. Hawaii is a blend of many cultures and nationalities.

3. What is the cause of the diverse lifestyle of Hawaii?

    _____

    _____

4. Which groups depend on the U.S. government for their living?

    _____

    _____

5. Which paragraphs include mostly facts and which mostly opinion?

    _____

    _____

People of the Rain Forests

People have lived in the rain forests for thousands of years. Many are farmers. Others are fishermen. Still others are hunters and gatherers. Some work outside their villages for part of the year, but mainly they depend on the forest for all of their needs.

1. What clues does the title tell you about the subject of this article? _____
   _____

2. What is the main idea of the paragraph? _____

3. In your own words, write three ideas that support the main idea. _____
   _____

4. Does this paragraph tell you where rain forests are? _____

The Dayak people live in the rain forest on the island of Borneo. Borneo is off the coast of Southeast Asia. Long ago the Dayak were hunters and gatherers who lived in thatched huts. Now they are settled farmers who grow rice and gather wild fruit. They hunt animals with blowpipes and poison darts. They are known for building bamboo suspension bridges. The Dayak population is estimated to be about 1 million.

1. What is the main idea of this paragraph? _____

2. In your own words, write three ideas that support the main idea. _____
   _____

3. The Dayak were once hunters and gatherers. Now they _____ .

4. What weapons do the Dayak use to hunt? _____

About 80,000 Huli people live in Papua New Guinea. They are farmers. Their main food is the sweet potato. They also grow sugar cane, bananas, corn, and pumpkins. Men and women live separate lives. Men live together in communal houses. Women live in individual huts with their children. They have gardens near their huts. Men cook and care for themselves.

1. What is the main idea of the paragraph? _____

2. In your own words, write three ideas that support the main idea. _____
   _____

3. How many crops do the Huli people grow?_____

4. Describe how Huli families live. _____
   _____

The Jivaro Indians live in Ecuador. The Jivaro plant corn, tobacco, beans, bananas, cotton, and cassava. They hunt with blowguns, spears, and darts. They fish with traps and raise llamas and guinea pigs. They were known for shrinking and preserving the heads of their enemies. About 10,000 Jivaro now live peacefullyin Ecuador.

1. What is the main idea of the paragraph? _____

2. In your own words, write three ideas that support the main idea. _____
   _____

3. Compare how the Jivaro Indians lived before and how they live now. Use a separate piece of paper.

4. What do you think is the most interesting fact about the Jivaro Indians? Use a separate piece of paper.

1. What does *mini* mean in the title word, *mini-ecosystem*?

_____

A Mini-Ecosystem

Bromeliads, plants that live on tree branches in the understory layer of the rain forests, are epiphytes. Epiphytes grow on trees instead of in soil. They are not parasites because they don't hurt the trees they live on. They are similar to orchids, mosses, and lichens.

2. List the epiphytes mentioned in the above paragraph.

_____

_____

Bromeliads get their nutrients from the air and water and from bits of dead algae and moss. This dead matter is called compost, which forms a thin layer on tree branches.

3. What is the main idea of this paragraph?

_____

_____

There is less light in the understory than in the canopy higher up. To adapt, bromeliads grow large leaves that point up to the light. The leaves are clustered so that rain falls into the center of the plant. A small pool of water collects there. Tree frogs lay their eggs in the pool, and tadpoles hatch. They swim in the center until they change into adult frogs. Insects hide in the bromeliad leaves. Birds and lizards drop by to find an insect meal.

4. What is the effect of the ability of bromeliads to collect a pool of water in its leaves?

_____

_____

5. Does this article say exactly what an ecosystem is? Using clues from the article, try to guess what an ecosystem is.

_____

_____

It's backbreaking work. All day long, we are bent over at the waist as we carefully replant our rice in the flooded paddy. But our feet tingle in the cool, rich, oozing mud.

1. Circle a compound word in this paragraph.

2. What is an antonym for *carefully*? _____

3. Which words describe how something feels on your skin? _____
_____

4. Where does this paragraph take place? _____

I don't think I can stand it any longer. I've got to tell Mom how much I dislike her asparagus custard pie. But how do I do it without hurting her feelings?

1. Which words have a hard **g** sound in the middle? _____

2. What word could you use instead of *dislike*? _____

3. What is the author's conflict? _____
_____

4. Think of a solution for the author. _____
_____

Lee and Kip were fighting again. Not with words. . .with fists. Jack was Kip's friend, and he knew he should stick up for him. But it wasn't Lee's fault that Kip was late for class three times this week. Jack hated fights. Between swings and kicks, Kip called, "Hey, Jack, are you with me or what?"

1. What two words make up the contraction in this paragraph? _____

2. What is the opposite of *late*? _____

3. What is Jack's conflict? _____

4. Think of a solution for Jack. _____

Mom gave me a choice. I could go with her and Dad to Aunt Terri's house. "She's always asking when you're going to come for a visit," Mom had said. Or, I could write letters to my relatives, inviting them to my birthday party. I really didn't want to do either one on my weekend.

1. What other vowel pair makes the same sound as the *oi* in *choice*? _____

2. What single word could you use instead of *always asking*? _____

3. What is the author's conflict? _____

4. Think of a solution for the author. _____

Score!

It was one of the closest games of the season. Neither team had been able to score, and time was running out. No score would mean overtime, but one good kick could mean winning the game.

Justin dashed down the soccer field toward the goal. "I'm open!" he shouted. "Pass the ball." He scanned the field around him, searching for a player from his team. "Brian, over here!"

Brian kicked the ball toward Justin, but before Justin could reach it, one of the opponents darted in and booted the ball away.

"Don't worry. We'll get it next time," yelled the coach as Brian sprinted back to regain possession of the ball.

This time, Brian dribbled out of the wing, beating opponent after opponent. He centered the ball, and Justin bolted up just in time to kick it toward the goal. It was caught by the goalie. The goalie threw the ball back into play.

The opponents now had possession of the ball. They flew past the first defender, took a shot at the goal, and missed. "Make this one count!" bellowed the goalie as he kicked the ball out to his team.

Brian was determined to score. The game was nearly over, but there was still no score on the board. He raced down the field. He could hear the fans in the background. "Go! Score!" they roared.

In a last effort, the whole team charged down to help him out. They passed the ball around the opponents and worked closer and closer to the goal. Justin passed the ball to Brian, who took aim at the goal and gave it a mighty kick. The shot was good! The team had won!

"Congratulations! You guys were great! What a game!" cheered the coach.

1. Fill in the blanks with homophones. Justin was _____ of the most

    determined players, so he was thrilled when his team _____ the game.

2. Justin and Brian keep trying to make the goal. They are

    a. lazy.

    b. discouraged.

    c. persistent.

3. List all the words in this story that describe someone moving quickly.

    _____

4. How many times do Justin and Brian team up to make the shot? _____

5. Write a different ending to this story. _____

    _____

Last-Minute Stardom

It was time for the play to begin, but the lead actress had not arrived. When the door opened, everyone looked up expecting to see Beth.

1. What clues does the title give you about what will happen in this writing?

   _____

2. What kind of writing is this: **fiction** or **nonfiction**? _____

3. What kind of fiction takes place in this story? _____

4. Use your own words to state the problem the first paragraph introduces.

   _____

Day #1

"I hate to put a damper on things, but Beth has a fever and cannot possibly make it tonight," explained her mom.

"Well, I never put all my eggs in one basket," responded Ms. King. "Amanda has been our understudy for that part and knows it well. Amanda, put on Beth's costume."

1. An idiom is an expression that means something different from what it actually says. List any idioms in this selection. _____

2. How did Ms. King respond to the problem? _____

3. Had Amanda worked hard as the understudy? _____

4. What clues from the paragraph helped you answer #3? _____

Day #2

Amanda was on cloud nine as she jumped off the stage after the performance and ran to where her family and friends were waiting at the back of the auditorium.

"You were terrific. You always were the apple of my eye," said Dad, as he gave Amanda a hug. Amanda was speechless as everyone complimented her.

1. List any idioms in this selection. _____

2. Was Amanda pleased with her performance? How do you know? _____

3. How did the "Last-Minute Stardom" happen? _____

4. Why do you think Amanda was speechless after the performance? _____

   _____

Day #3

Dad said, "It's raining cats and dogs outside. Grandpa, keep an eye on everyone while I run and get the car."

Finally Dad returned. "Sorry it took so long. The traffic is slower than molasses in January. I avoided an accident in the parking lot only by the skin of my teeth."

1. List any idioms in this selection. _____

2. What members of Amanda's family were at the performance? _____

3. What lesson could you take away after reading this story? _____

   _____

4. Write a lesson someone could learn from this story. _____

Day #4

1. Does the title give any specific information about the subject of this piece? Is the title an idiom?

_____

Lay It on the Line

We were having a good time in the school hallway when out of the clear blue sky Jana started up. I knew it! She just had to ask me about my trip to Jamaica. Oh shoot, she really had me over a barrel. Man! I wanted to fly the coop. You see, a couple days before, I had lied about going to Jamaica. Sure, Jana's been there, but not me! It seems I can't hold a candle to her when it comes to interesting vacations to brag about.

2. An idiom is an expression that means something different from what it actually says. Match the idioms in this paragraph with the literal meaning below.

am greatly inferior   _____

without warning   _____

escape   _____

helpless; at a disadvantage _____

"Why, Dougie," Jana teased. "What's wrong? Cat got your tongue?" She smiled roguishly at me.

Boy, that girl sure hit the nail on the head with that question. And then she nagged me all day.

3. Write your own literal meaning for the two idioms in the section above.

_____

I warned her to cool it. You can't imagine how angry she makes me. Shoot! She didn't listen though. She really had a one-track mind! I was a sitting duck to her digs and verbal jabs. Then she started bragging about all her trips around the world! And the rest of the class was all ears to anything she'd say. In a nutshell, that girl is and always will be too big for her britches!

4. How many sentences end with an exclamation point? What does that tell you about how the author feels?

_____

5. What do you think is the real cause of Dougie's problem: his lie about going to Jamaica or Jana traveling around the world? Explain.

_____

_____

Clara Brown was born a slave. Slaves were given their owner's last name. Clara's owner, George Brown, bought her in 1835. Her family was auctioned off to different owners. Slave traders bought her husband and son. Her daughters went to two different owners. Clara lost touch with all of her family.

1. What sound does the *ti* in *auction* make?_____

2. What is the opposite of *bought*? _____

3. What is the main idea of this paragraph?_____

4. How do you think it made Clara feel to be without her family? _____

_____

Day #1

The 1850 census showed about 4 million African Americans living in the United States. Of the 4 million, 400,000 were free. Free African Americans had to obey laws established for them. They weren't allowed to socialize with slaves. Nor could they hold meetings.

1. What word has the same consonant sound in the beginning, middle, and end._____

2. Write out the number 400,000._____

3. What fraction of African Americans were free in 1850? _____

4. Why do you think free African Americans couldn't associate with slaves?

_____

Day #2

Clara got her freedom papers in 1857. African Americans had to carry their papers at all times to prove they weren't runaway slaves. Clara wanted to go West to search for her daughter Eliza. A wagon master offered her a job as a cook on his wagon train. Clara took the job and moved to Denver.

1. What is the root of *freedom*?_____

2. What other word could you use instead of *got* in the first sentence? _____

3. What might have been the effect if Clara Brown had lost her freedom papers?

_____

4. Why do you think Clara had to get a job on her way out West? _____

Day #3

Clara began doing laundry. She charged 50 cents a shirt. After five years, Clara owned property worth $10,000.

After the Civil War, Clara went back to Kentucky to look for her daughter. There she helped pay for 16 ex-slaves to go to Colorado. Finally, in 1882, Clara was reunited with her daughter.

1. Find a word with a silent consonant pair. _____

2. What does *reunited* mean? What, then, does the prefix *re-* mean? _____

3. How many washed shirts does $10,000 represent?_____

4. Was Clara generous with her money? What clues help you answer that question?

_____

Day #4

Assessment

Clara Brown and the Wagon Train

Clara Brown was born a slave. She got her freedom papers in 1857. Clara had one year to leave the state. If she didn't leave, the law said she would become a slave again.

In 1859, African Americans could not buy tickets for public transportation. Passage on a wagon train cost about $500. Clara wanted to go West to search for her daughter Eliza. A wagon master offered her a job as a cook on his wagon train. Clara took the job.

Clara began cooking each morning at 4 A.M. Travel began by 7 A.M. The wagon train stopped for a break at noon and started traveling again at 2 P.M. Wagons rolled until 5 P.M. Oxen pulled the wagons. Oxen were cheaper than horses or mules. Oxen cost about $50 apiece, half the price of a mule. Oxen pulled a loaded wagon at about 2 mph (about 3 kph) on flat land. A wagon train traveled about 15 miles (about 24 km) a day. A train had 30 to 200 wagons. Each wagon carried up to 2,500 pounds (1,193 kg). It took Clara's wagon train about eight weeks to get to Denver from Kansas. The trip was about 680 miles (about 1,094 km). Clara walked the whole way.

1. Find a word with a silent consonant in the middle. _____

2. What is the plural of *ox*? _____

3. What is the main idea of the first paragraph?

    a. Clara was home free when she got her freedom papers.

    b. Clara got her freedom papers in 1857, but she had to leave the state or risk becoming a slave again.

    c. Clara lost her freedom papers.

4. How many minutes (or hours) do you usually walk a day? Compare that with how many hours a day Clara walked on the journey to Denver.

    _____

    _____

5. Why did Clara get a job on her way out West? Compare your answer here with your answer to the same question earlier this week.

    _____

    _____

James Beckwourth and Fur Trading

Lewis and Clark's exploration led to fur trading in the West. Several companies competed with each other for trade. The companies sold pelts in markets around the world. They had to hire men to get furs for them. The trappers, who trapped deer, beaver, and muskrat, became known as the mountain men. People of different races worked together in the fur trade.

1. What does the title tell you about the subject of this article?_____

2. What job do you think James Beckwourth had?_____

3. An equal opportunity employer will treat an employee without regard to his or her race. Was the fur trade an equal opportunity employer? _____

4. What clues from the paragraph helped you answer #3?_____

Day #1

One of those men was an African American named James Beckwourth. His mother was a slave. He was born in Virginia but grew up in Missouri. His father taught him to ride horses, shoot, work the land, cook, fish, and track game. He apprenticed to a blacksmith for five years. In 1818, when he was 20 years old, he began exploring the West.

1. How old was James when he became apprenticed to the blacksmith?_____

2. Name three skills James's father taught him. _____

3. Why do you think James's father taught him those things?_____

4. Which parts of the country (not the name of the state) did James live in over the course of his life? _____

Day #2

James lived with Native American tribes, and from them he learned how to trap beaver and otter. In 1823, he worked as a scout for a fur company. In 1824, he married a Crow woman named Pine Leaf.

1. When the author says James married a Crow woman, what does that mean?
   a. She looked like a crow.
   b. She was a member of the Native American Crow tribe.
   c. She raised crows.

2. What were the effects of James living with Native American tribes?_____

3. Does this paragraph tell you what happens to beavers after they're trapped? _____

4. What do you think a fur company does to a beaver after it is trapped?_____

Day #3

James became a famous mountain man. He found a pass through the Sierra Nevadas, now known as Beckwourth Pass. It was an important route for wagon trains going to California.

1. In what mountain range would you find Beckwourth Pass? _____

2. What jobs did Beckwourth hold? Use information from the entire article. _____

   _____

3. Do you consider James Beckwourth a hero? Why or why not?_____

   _____

4. Would you like to have had James Beckwourth's life? Why or why not? _____

   _____

Day #4

Assessment

1. What do you picture when you see the title "Cowboys"?

_____

Cowboys

In 1865, at the end of the Civil War, there were only five western states: Texas, Nevada, Oregon, Kansas, and Oklahoma. There were few towns in those states. Native Americans lived in western lands, but most of the land was still unsettled.

Slaves needed jobs after the war. At first, they went to Texas to work on cattle ranches. They called the road to Texas the Freedom Road.

From the 1870s to the 1890s, one out of every five cowboys was African American. Some saved enough money to buy their own small ranches and cattle.

2. Why did the ex-slaves call the road to Texas the Freedom Road? _____

_____

Nat Love was born into a slave family in Tennessee. In 1869, he traveled to Dodge City, Kansas, hoping to become a cowboy. He drove cattle from Texas to Dodge City every spring and summer. Nat worked with both Caucasian and African American cowboys. Nat was skilled in roping, riding, and taming wild horses. During a rodeo in 1876 in South Dakota, he won every event. Other cowboys called him Deadwood Dick because of his expert shooting.

3. Was Nat Love good at being a cowboy? What clues from the paragraph helped you answer that question?_____

_____

George McJunkin was born a slave in Texas. From Spanish cowboys on his owner's ranch, he learned how to rope and ride horses. After the Civil War, he went to New Mexico. There he worked on ranches as a trail driver. He was skilled in breaking, or taming, wild horses. He became a wagon boss for two ranches. He was responsible for 200 horses, 1,000 cattle, and 100 Caucasian cowboys. He had always been interested in archeology. He liked to hunt for fossils. One day he discovered the fossils of an ancient bison containing a spear point. The fossils were found to be at least 10,000 years old. His discovery proved that people lived in North America far longer than anyone had believed.

4. What clues from the paragraph tell you that George McJunkin had a curious mind? _____

_____

5. What different groups of people were cowboys? _____

_____

Mrs. Candy Gramme, the sixth-grade English teacher, gave her class an assignment to write a poem. "Write about something you like. Perhaps this beautiful day. Perhaps a sport you enjoy playing or watching. Perhaps a person you admire or adore."

1. Which word has a silent letter in the middle?_____

2. What other word could you use instead of *perhaps*? _____

3. Think of something else to write a poem about. _____

4. How many suggestions does Mrs. Gramme give her students? _____

_____

Day #1

"Oh boy!" moaned a despondent Madeline. She didn't have a clue what to choose for a poetry topic. Sitting glumly at the dining room table that evening, unable to focus on a central theme, Madeline became distracted by her baby sister.

"Hey, you little squirt! You're my inspiration!" she laughed. And away she wrote.

1. What other word in the paragraph has the same vowel sound as the *oo* in *choose*? _____

2. What other word could you use instead of *despondent*? _____

3. What is a central theme? _____

4. When and where does Madeline work on her homework?_____

Day #2

When Betsy first did grace us with her charm,
I'd promised Mom I'd keep her from all harm.
I'd hold her tightly, rocking her at night,
To scare away the goblins that would fright.

1. List all the words that rhyme. _____

2. What does *grace us* mean? _____

3. If you were reading the third verse out loud, what actions might you do to emphasize the words? _____

4. Have you had a baby brother or sister? If so, how did you feel about him or her at first?

_____

Day #3

Then came those diapers, noxious with their smell.
Warm baby food ensmearing face as well
As floor, wall, me! "This babe's a creepy snake
Of sin!" I cried. "She's keeping me awake!"

Yet anger flees. My heart cries all a'thrill

When in my arms she nestles, cuddly still.

1. Rewrite the *x* in *noxious* so it reflects how the *x* is pronounced. _____

2. What does *noxious* mean in this verse? _____

3. Why would Madeline exaggerate and call Betsy a "creepy snake"? _____

_____

4. Compare Madeline's state of mind in stanzas 2 and 3. _____

Day #4

Pen Pals

Dear Yena,

My name is Li Lui. I am ten years old. I live in Beijing, China. My parents and I live in a tall apartment building. Beijing is a busy city with crowded sidewalks and lots to do.

I attend school from 7:00 A.M. until 4:30 P.M. My favorite subjects are art and Chinese. I don't like math at all, but I have to study it every day! When I grow up, I want to be a fashion designer.

I love drawing, watching TV, and eating. My favorite shows are cartoons. My favorite food is shrimp chips. We eat a lot of rice, fish, and vegetables. We eat fish for breakfast to start the day with protein for strength. I like to drink soda.

I'm glad to have a pen pal from another country. I hope you are having a nice day! Please write soon.

> Sincerely,
>
> Li Lui

Dear Li Lui,

Thank you for writing! I am excited to have a pen pal from China. I live in Accra, the capital of Ghana. My home is a one-floor house on a quiet street. I live with my parents and grandmother.

My favorite school subject is science. I want to be a pediatrician when I grow up so I can help heal sick children. I'm not so good at French. I need to practice more, but I find it so dull!

My favorite television programs are cartoons, too. Maybe we watch the same shows. I love to eat plantains. They're similar to bananas. I could eat them all day! I eat a lot of rice, also. I like fruit juice better than soda, though.

We have lots in common! I hope you are doing well, and I look forward to your reply.

> Sincerely,
>
> Yena

1. What is the silent letter in *Ghana*? _____

2. What is a pediatrician? _____

3. Make and fill in a comparison chart with these categories: kind of house, family members, favorite school subject, least favorite school subject, favorite TV show, general diet, favorite food, favorite drink, future job.

4. Based on your chart, is it true that Li Liu and Yena have a lot in common? Explain. _____

5. Which girl's life would you rather *not* have? Why? _____

Farmer Questions Chicken IQ

Hengaard, North Dakota—A poultry farmer in this remote community 50 miles west of Bismark made a startling discovery last Thursday as he inspected one of his hen coops. His chickens were raising their own livestock.

1. What kind of writing is this? _____

2. In the title, what does _IQ_ mean? _____

3. What is the "startling discovery"? _____

4. Why do you think it was it startling? _____

Day #1

"In one corner of the coop, the biddies had set up a box of beetles," said Bert DeHaan. "I guess they've fed them (beetles) grain from their own mix. Can't say I ever saw anything like it before. No, this is a real corker."

According to Shannon Scratch, inspector for the state agriculture administration, the chickens had also developed a cockroach ranch, an ant colony, and a mealworm pit.

1. Two people are interviewed in this article. Who are they? _____

2. Why are they interviewed? _____

3. How many kinds of livestock were the chickens raising? _____

4. What is another way to say a _real corker_? _____

Day #2

Mr. DeHaan says, "The chickens are raising the bugs for food. No doubt about it. I've seen them herd them, separate the fattened critters, and gobble them down like they were having a feast." Records show that egg production in this coop has improved by 23% in the past 18 months, far above the production of other coops.

1. Why does the farmer think the chickens are doing this? _____

2. What evidence does Mr. DeHaan present to back that up? _____
   _____

3. Has the farmer noticed any benefit to this chicken behavior? If so, what? _____

4. Are these chickens being raised for their eggs or for meat? _____

Day #3

When asked how smart his flock was, DeHaan smiled and shrugged his shoulders. "Don't know for sure, but can't be as dumb as some folks around here. You know, there's been talk of an alien landing around these parts..."

1. What does Mr. DeHaan suggest is the cause of this startling chicken behavior?
   _____

2. Do you think that's the likely cause? Why or why not? _____
   _____

3. What is the main idea of this article? _____

4. What happens to the main idea if it turns out that the farmer faked the whole thing? _____

Day #4

Assessment

1. What does the title tell you about what kind of writing this will be?

    _____

Letter to My Teacher

Dear Mrs. Brewton,

Aloha from the big island! This state is so beautiful. We had the chance to drive fairly close to the volcano again this week, and then we went to a great luau. I'm learning a lot about the land, people, and wildlife here. I never thought I'd see some of the rocks and plants you talked about in class.

2. Read between the lines to figure out where the writer is living this summer. How do you know? _____

    _____

I've met a few more kids this past week. I've made a lot of friends since school ended in June. By the way, how are things in North Country? Any news from those friendly Americans to your south? The kids here think we only play hockey and race dogsleds. They were stunned to find out I love to kick the old ball around. I don't get to play fullback or goalie as much as I do back home, but it's still good practice for being on the team again next fall.

3. Read between the lines to figure out where the writer is from. How do you know? _____

    _____

Say, before I forget, how is Fletch doing? Thanks for taking care of him while I'm gone. Let me know what you think of his coloring. It seems to me his green feathers are a bit less glossy than they should be. Although I miss him and he misses me (he does call me "Lady Love," you know), I know he's in good hands. Just don't teach him too many new words. His vocabulary is already greater than most of our class!

I'll see you next fall.

With great appreciation,

Chris

4. Read between the lines to figure out what kind of pet Chris owns. How do you know? _____

    _____

5. Read between the lines to figure out whether Chris is a girl or a boy. How do you know? _____

    _____

Castles were the center of feudal life in the Middle Ages. Conflicts were common, so castles were well protected by a strong military, high walls, moats, and sometimes surrounding high mountains. Inside the castle walls, lords, ladies, servants and staff, priests, soldiers, and animals lived safely protected from their enemies.

1. How else could you write the same sound as the *feu* in *feudal*? _____

2. What word could you use instead of *military*? _____

3. What was the effect of the many conflicts in the Middle Ages? _____

4. What was the purpose of the castle? _____

Day #1

The castle's defense included thick stone walls with tall round towers at the corners. Soldiers kept watch for enemies from the top of the towers. Battlements atop the towers protected the soldiers. They hurled arrows or rocks through the spaces between the stone uprights, called merlons.

1. Is the *ie* in *enemies* pronounced like the *ie* in **flies** or **jellies**? _____

2. What is a *merlon*? _____

3. What shape is a tower usually? _____

4. What was the job of a soldier? _____
   _____

Day #2

Since the tower was often the strongest structure, many of the castle's residents lived within its walls. The servants' and soldiers' quarters were on the first floor. The second level served as the secure sleeping quarters of the lord and his family. The basement held the wells and was used as a storehouse. Even if an enemy repeatedly attacked the castle, its residents could survive a long siege in the tower with its thick walls, water, and storage of food.

1. Is the *ie* in *siege* pronounced like the *ie* in **enemies** or **tries**? _____

2. What is a siege? _____

3. What is the topic of this paragraph?
   a. sieges   b. sleeping quarters   c. castle towers

4. Why did the lord and his family live in the tower? _____

Day #3

Serfs and peasants were poor people who lived in or around the castle. They provided services or farmed to support the castle. In return, the lords provided them with a small piece of land, protection in wartime, and a local government to settle disputes among them.

1. What word is a homophone of *serfs*? _____

2. What is a *dispute*? _____

3. What is the main topic of this paragraph? _____

4. Did serfs always live in the castle? _____

Day #4

Castle Days

Knights and soldiers were trained warriors who were given land in exchange for protection of the castle. Knights and their horses dressed in heavy, protective armor made of iron. When they were not in battles, jousting kept them active. Jousting was a combat between two armed knights on horses carrying lances.

The rulers were wealthy lords and ladies, or royalty, who built the castle to defend their land. They were expected to treat soldiers and those who served them with honor. Lords often acted as judges and presided over the feudal court under strict codes of behavior. Life in a castle could be exciting for its rulers.

The castle social life revolved around the great hall. It contained the kitchen, chapel, and garderobes (toilets), with a huge warming fire in the center. Fancy medieval feasts were celebrated here. Lords and ladies danced and listened to minstrels. On special occasions, entertainment included a joust.

Only a few castles containing the relics of medieval days stand intact. However, the ruins of many castles can still be found in Europe. Suits of armor, authentic weapons, and beautiful castle tapestries are displayed in museums around the world today.

1. Which letters are silent in *knights*?_____

2. What is jousting?_____
   _____

3. Use one to three words each to describe the main topic for each of the four paragraphs.

   _____
   _____
   _____
   _____

4. What are the two purposes of a joust?_____
   _____

5. Compare a medieval feast with your idea of a great feast.

   _____
   _____

Robin Hood: Was He Real?

Ballads were storytelling songs popular in the fourteenth and fifteenth centuries. In the Middle Ages, singing poets called minstrels performed ballads in castles and in villages. English ballads told of Robin Hood.

1. Based on the title, whom will this piece be about? _____

2. Based on the title, what question is the author going to talk about?_____
_____

3. Have you heard of Robin Hood? _____

4. If so, do you think he was a real person?_____

Robin Hood was an outlaw who lived in Sherwood Forest. He was a hero of the common people. Robin Hood robbed from the rich and gave to the poor. He fought the Sheriff of Nottingham, a corrupt official who harassed the poor.

1. What is an outlaw? _____

2. Who are the common people: the **rich** or the **poor**? _____

3. What example does the author give to demonstrate what it means to be a corrupt official? _____

4. Given this description, do you think Robin Hood is a hero? Why or why not?
_____

Robin Hood had a merry band of followers. They were Friar Tuck, a fat, jolly priest; Little John, who was more than seven feet tall and very skilled with a bow and arrow; Will Scarlet; and Maid Marian, who was Robin's sweetheart.

1. Do you think Robin Hood and his band of followers had a good time robbing the rich and giving to the poor?_____

2. What clues from the paragraph helped you answer #1?_____

3. What fact about Little John is surprising, given his name? _____

4. Were all Robin Hood's followers men? _____

Some scholars say Robin Hood existed. They believe he was the Earl of Huntington, whose real name was Robert Fitzooth. Robin Hood was the subject of children's books, movies, and television programs in the twentieth century.

1. Does everyone agree that Robin Hood is a fictional person? _____

2. What clues from the paragraph helped you answer #1?_____

3. How is the story of Robin Hood told today? _____

4. Why do you think the story of Robin Hood is still interesting today? _____
_____

Assessment

1. What does the title tell you about the subject of this article and about the issue being discussed?

_____

King Arthur: Was He Real?

Many popular stories were told about King Arthur and his knights. The first stories were oral, but later they were written down. The oral stories changed as they were retold. Writers have been writing about King Arthur for about a thousand years. Their stories tell of his brave deeds and of the adventures of the Knights of the Round Table.

2. What sentence in the paragraph contains a clue that the stories about King Arthur might not be very accurate?

_____

In the stories, King Arthur was the son of Uther Pendragon, king of Britain. Arthur grew up not knowing he was of royal ancestry. But he was the only person able to pull the magic sword Excalibur from a block of stone. Many people before him had tried unsuccessfully. His success proved he was heir to the throne of Britain, so he became king. Arthur was a wise and strong ruler. His queen was Guinevere. Arthur had many knights in his court. They included Gawain, Lancelot, Kay, Percival, and Galahad. His court was in Camelot. Arthur's knights sat at a round table built to show that they were all equal.

3. What was the cause of Arthur becoming king?

_____

Arthur fought in Europe against the Roman Empire, but he was called home because his nephew seized his kingdom. In a final battle, they both fell, stabbed by each other's swords. Arthur was taken to the island of Avalon to heal.

Some historians believe Arthur was a mythological character. Others believe he was based on a real British leader who fought battles with German invaders in the early 500s.

No matter whether King Authur was real or not, the ballads contain valuable information about the ideas and social conditions in medieval England.

4. If Robin Hood stories are set around the 1200s, and King Arthur stories are set around the early 500s, how much older are King Arthur stories?

_____

_____

5. Which is more important about the ballads: whether King Arthur was a real person or the information they provide about medieval life? Why?

_____

_____

Ralph was a dirty mutt. His once-white hair was gray and brown with grime. He wore a black collar around his neck that had once been blue. On the dirty collar hung an identification tag, if anyone could get close enough to read it.

1. Circle the word that has a middle sound like *but*.

2. Circle a word the writer uses instead of *dirt*.

3. What is Ralph? _____

4. What details in the paragraph helped you decide this? _____

_____

Right now, Ralph was on his belly. He inched forward under the lilac bushes. His long hair dragged in the dirt. His bright, black eyes were glued on a plate at the edge of the table. On it was a ham sandwich. His moist, black nose twitched with the smell.

1. Circle the word that starts and ends with the same sound.

2. What does *moist* mean? _____

3. Is Ralph moving quickly or slowly? _____

4. Predict what will happen next. _____

I said, "It's time for bed." That announcement triggered a running marathon all through the house until I cornered Bart in the living room closet. I carried him up to his bedroom, and, amazingly, he fell asleep almost immediately.

1. Circle the words with two or more letters that begin with a short **a** sound.

2. Does the word *marathon* tell us that the writer chased Bart for a long time or a short time? _____

3. What was the effect on Bart when the writer announced that it was bedtime?

_____

4. Is the writer surprised that Bart fell asleep so quickly? _____

"The house looks great!" said Mrs. Bradford. "Can you come back tomorrow?"

"Uh ... I don't think so, Mrs. Bradford. I'm pretty busy until next year—I mean next week."

While I lay in bed that night, I thought that someone had reversed a couple of letters in Bart's name.

1. If you undo the contraction *I'm*, what does it say? _____

2. What does *reversed* mean? _____

3. What word does the author think Bart's name should be? _____

4. What job do you think the writer has? _____

Summer Storm

Brian went zooming to the park on his bike. It started out as a perfect day, until Brian's mom made him drag his little brother Pete along.

"Wait for me, Brian," whined Pete as he tried to keep up.

Brian parked his bike and followed his nose to the concession stand. There were sizzling burgers on the grill, fresh-popped popcorn, and big barrels of fizzing root beer. He made his purchase and handed Pete his lunch. "Sit here and eat, and don't move until I come back to get you," Brian said.

As Pete began eating, he heard the pitter-patter of rain falling around him, but he stayed dry under the large tree. As the rain increased, the wind began to howl. With the leaves rustling above his head, it sounded as though it was raining harder. Then he heard the plink of the hail on the roof of the concession stand. When Pete saw lightning in the distance, he knew he should move from under the tree. Brian would just have to look for him.

When the storm got worse, Brian knew he had to find Pete. Brian thought he heard his name as he ran but then wondered if it was the wind playing tricks on him. There it was again. "Brian!" That voice had never sounded so good.

1. Find a word that has two *c*'s in it, each pronounced a different way.

   _____

2. What happened to the rain when it increased?_____

   _____

3. This story is full of words whose sounds make you think of what they mean, such as zooming and fizzing. Words like these are examples of onomatopoeia. Use the clues to write the correct word from the story on the line. Each word will be an example of onomatopoeia.

   a. moving rapidly _____

   b. sharp, metallic sound _____

   c. a series of light, quick, tapping sounds _____

4. Write clues for two other examples of onomatopoeia used in the story.

   _____

   _____

5. Why was it a good decision for Pete to leave the tree during the lightning storm?

   _____

   _____

The Story of the Cherokee Rose

In 1838, the government of the United States made the Cherokees move from their homes in Georgia and other states to what was then called the Indian Territory. That land is now the state of Oklahoma.

1. What clues does the title give us about the subject of this article? _____

2. Does the first paragraph tell us anything about who the Cherokees were? _____

3. Does the first paragraph tell us anything about the rose in the title? _____

4. How long ago did the events in this story take place? _____

_____

The Cherokees had to walk for hundreds of miles, and they often did not have enough food or water. Many hundreds of them died. The mothers felt so sad that some of them could not take care of their children.

1. How did the Cherokees get to Indian Territory? _____

2. Does the author include any opinions in this paragraph? _____

3. Who is feeling sad in this paragraph? _____

4. This trip is called the Trail of Tears. What clues tell you why? _____

_____

According to the legend, the chiefs asked the Great One for a sign that would make the mothers feel better and make them strong enough to take care of their children.

1. Who in the tribe came up with a solution to the problem? _____

2. What solution did the tribe come up with for the mothers? _____

3. Who do you think the Great One was? _____

4. If you were the Great One, what kind of sign would you send to make the mothers feel better and be stronger? _____

_____

The Great One promised that where a mother's tear fell, a flower would grow. That flower is called the Cherokee rose. It is white, which stands for the mothers' tears. The flower's center is gold, a symbol of the gold that was taken from the tribes' land. The seven leaves on the rose's stem stand for the seven groups of people that walked along the Trail of Tears.

1. What is the Cherokee rose? _____

2. How does the story say the Cherokee rose comes about? _____

3. What are the different parts of the rose, and what are they symbols of? You may want to make a chart.

4. How does this story make you feel? _____

Day #1

Day #2

Day #3

Day #4

55

1. Without looking back on your earlier work, what do you remember about the Trail of Tears? _____

_____

The Trail of Tears

The ancient Cherokee were hunters and farmers. They lived in the area that we know as the Appalachian Mountains of Georgia. But in 1829, white settlers found gold on this land. They went to the United States government and asked that the Cherokee be forced to leave the land, hoping they would then get the rights to it.

2. Why did the settlers want the Cherokee to leave? _____

_____

A new law called the Indian Removal Act of 1830 was passed. The law stated that all Native Americans east of the Mississippi would be moved. They would have to move to an Indian territory in the west, an area in what is now Oklahoma.

3. Were the settlers successful? _____

_____

Some agreed to go, but most would not leave their land. Starting in the spring of 1838, the army gathered the Cherokee together. The people were held in forts like prisoners. Within one month, the first group of Cherokee was forced to leave Georgia. They marched over 1,000 miles to the new land. Some people had horses and wagons. Most people walked. The trip lasted many months. Thousands died, either during the march or once they got to the land. There was no shelter or food at the territory. The last group of Cherokee arrived on the Indian Territory in March of 1839. In all, almost 17,000 Cherokee were forced to move to the new land.

4. Did the Cherokee go willingly? _____

5. Do you think it was a fair trade: thousands of dead and displaced Cherokees for a chance to mine gold? Why or why not? .

_____

_____

Each year, the citizens of the United States celebrate two holidays to remember servicemen and women who fought in wars to preserve citizens' freedom. On November 11, Veterans Day is celebrated, and on the last Monday in May, Memorial Day is celebrated.

1. What is the silent consonant pair in this paragraph? _____

2. What is a synonym for *celebrated* as it is used here: **partied** or **observed**? _____

3. Which sentence is the topic sentence? _____

4. Which holiday has a date that is relative (the date we observe it depends on another factor)?

_____

Day #1

On November 11, 1918, a treaty was signed between the Germans and the Allied forces of the United States, France, Great Britain, Russia, and Italy, putting an end to World War I. It was first called Armistice Day, but it is now called Veterans Day. George Honey, an Australian journalist, asked the whole world to remain silent for two minutes as the treaty was signed. Even the radios were silent.

1. How do you pronounce the *ss* in *Russia*? _____

2. What does *armistice* mean?
   a. beginning of war   b. declaration of the winner of the battle   c. parties agree to end war

3. If you read the second sentence of this paragraph out loud, which two words would you emphasize? _____

4. Can one person make a difference in how the whole world behaves? What details from the paragraph helped you answer that question? _____

Day #2

Memorial Day began after the Civil War, when people began decorating the graves of soldiers who had died in the war. Although many claim to have started the tradition, Congress declared Waterloo, New York, the birthplace of Memorial Day when the whole community held a celebration on May 5, 1866.

1. Find a compound word in this paragraph. _____

2. What is a grave? _____

3. Which holiday is older: **Memorial Day** or **Veterans Day**? _____

4. How many years older is that holiday? _____

Day #3

In 1868, the Grand Army of the Republic organized a ceremony at the National Cemetery in Arlington, Virginia. They called it Decoration Day because they decorated the graves of soldiers. The holiday stuck, but the name was changed to Memorial Day. On this day, many communities hold parades in remembrance of servicemen and women who gave their lives for the freedom of the United States.

1. Find an example of alliteration in this paragraph. _____

2. What word is the opposite of *freedom*? _____

3. Restate the last sentence in your own words. _____

4. Do you think we should combine the two holidays into one? Why or why not? _____

_____

Day #4

The Statue of Liberty

The Statue of Liberty is a symbol of freedom and welcome to the world. Frédéric Bartholdi of France sculpted the statue. It was a gift from France to the United States. The statue symbolized friendship between the two countries. It was also intended to honor the birthday of the United States' independence. President Grover Cleveland dedicated the statue in 1886. It became a national monument in 1924. The statue is located on Liberty Island in New York Harbor.

The original name for the statue was "Liberty Enlightening the World." The statue's torch is a welcome symbol to immigrants. It's Liberty's way of enlightening the world. The crown has seven rays. They symbolize the seven oceans and the seven continents. Liberty has a tablet in her left hand. It shows the date July 4, 1776. The broken chain at her feet symbolizes freedom. Her Greek robe symbolizes Greece as the birthplace of democracy.

Liberty stands on a pedestal. Americans had to raise money to pay for the pedestal. Joseph Pulitzer was editor of *The World*, a New York newspaper. He thought the statue was a great idea. His newspaper ran articles about raising money for the statue. He published the names of people who gave money. He even listed the names of children who sent pennies. Americans raised $250,000. That was enough money to pay for the pedestal. The French people paid for the statue.

1. What are the prefix, root, and suffix in *Enlightening*? _____

_____

2. What is a symbol?

   a. an image that stands for an idea

   b. a part of a drum kit

   c. a statue

3. What is the main idea of paragraph 2? _____

_____

4. What is the symbol for the oceans and continents? _____

5. Imagine you were a kid in the 1880s. Do you think you would've sent in pennies to pay for the pedestal? Why or why not? _____

_____

Slumber Party

It was the night Annabel had looked forward to for weeks! Four girls were arriving for a sleepover party. Finally, four cars pulled up and the doorbell rang. Annabel threw open the door and welcomed her guests. The girls piled into Annabel's house in a jumble of sleeping bags and overnight cases.

1. What clues does the title give you about the subject of this story? _____

2. What is another way to say *slumber party*? _____

3. Do you imagine that kids get a lot of sleep at a slumber party? _____

4. How many girls in all are at the party? _____

Thank you for inviting me," Robin replied. "I brought you a thank-you gift." She held out a small box to her hostess.

"Yum! Chocolates!" Sheila shouted. She grabbed the box and shoved a candy into her mouth. She dropped the empty wrapper on the floor. "Got any milk?" she said, with her mouth full.

1. Which word describes Robin?   a. fearful   b. greedy   c. polite

2. Write two examples of Robin's behavior from the story to prove why your description fits.
   _____

3. Which word describes Sheila?   a. rude   b. fearful   c. gracious

4. Write two examples of Sheila's behavior from the story to prove why your description fits.
   _____

Annabel noticed that one of her guests did not look happy. "Tamiko, what's wrong?"

"I've never slept away from home," Tamiko admitted. "I'm a little nervous."

"You'll be all right," Annabel reassured her. "But, you can use the phone to call home if you need to. It's right over there . . . Hey? Where's the phone?"

1. Which word describes Tamiko?   a. fearful   b. rude   c. greedy

2. Write two examples of Tamiko's behavior from the story to prove why your description fits.
   _____

3. What advice would you give Tamiko to help her get over her nervousness? _____

4. Does this paragraph tell you anything about what time of year this story takes place? _____

Paula had the phone. "Is it okay if Dan comes over?" She called to Annabel. "He is bored."

"No!" Annabel responded, a little shocked. "There are no boys at this slumber party."

"Oh." Paula rolled her eyes and went back to chatting on the phone.

1. Which word describes Paula?   a. gracious b. rude   c. polite

2. Write two examples of Paula's behavior from the story to prove why your description fits.
   _____

3. Compare each girl's behavior. What is the first thing each girl did after walking through the door? _____

4. Girls: Which kind of guest do you think you would be more like? Boys: If there were a girls' slumber party at your house, what would you do? _____

 0-7682-3215-5 *Read 4 Today*

Day #1

Day #2

Day #3

Day #4

1. What kind of writing will this be?

_____

Ben's Journal

February 9

Tomorrow is the big day. I've studied so hard for the past three weeks that I think I could spell these words in my sleep.

But what if I get nervous and mess up? What if someone else knows more words than I know? Rebecca always wins when we practice at school. I just want to do the best that I can.

Mom has helped me every night after supper. She says that studying and learning are more important, in the long run, than winning. I guess she's right. But I still really hope I win.

2. Circle the words that best describe how Ben was feeling the day before the event.

confident   tired   anxious   happy

February 10

I did it! Well, I didn't win first place, but I came in second. And I'm really proud of that.

At first, I was scared when I looked out and saw all those people in the audience. I was afraid I'd forget everything. But then I told myself, "You studied hard. You know all those words. Come on, you can do it!"

3. What was Ben's strategy to getting over his nervousness?_____

_____

My first word was *indicate*: i-n-d-i-c-a-t-e. It was easy. Then I knew I could do the rest of them, too. The only word that really stumped me was *cannibal*. I spelled it c-a-n-n-i-b-l-e—oops. Rebecca spelled it right, along with her last word: *hydraulics*.

Oh well, I won a dictionary and had my picture taken for the newspaper. When I came home, my family had a party to celebrate! Tomorrow, I start studying for next year's contest.

4. How did Ben feel about winning second place?

    a. upset because he didn't win first place
    b. happy because he did his best
    c. angry at the person who beat him

5. What do you think will happen next year at the spelling contest? Write a journal entry from Ben's point of view about what might happen.

My favorite blood-pumping, wholly invigorating game was King of the Mountain. You see, one player would dash up the hillock, pose menacingly at the top, and claim, "King of the Mountain!" Then the attackers would pull, push, or tackle to dethrone the king. Whoever next reached the lofty heights would exclaim, "King of the Mountain!" And the game would start anew.

1. Does the **c** in *menacingly* have the same beginning sound as **king** or **sing**? _____

2. What is the prefix in *dethrone*? What does *dethrone* mean?_____

3. There are some great adjectives in this paragraph. List them. _____

_____

4. Does this game sound like it has a lot of rules? _____

Day #1

School teachers frowned on the game. And for good reason. Bloody noses, arguing combatants, torn clothing, and broken spectacles resulted in phone calls from concerned parents and, consequently, a new "Thou Shalt Not . . ." rule in the school playground rules book. No, school was no place for this sport.

1. Does the first syllable of *combatants* sound more like **come** or **comb**? _____

2. What are combatants? _____

3. There is a chain of cause and effect in sentence 3 of this paragraph. Restate it briefly in your own words._____

4. Does the author agree with the school rule that they are not allowed to play King of the Mountain? _____

Day #2

So we played King of the Mountain after school hours on other turf. No supervision. Most parents averted their eyes, crossed their fingers, and prayed for swift healing for whatever injuries would surely occur. Pretty cool. Pretty naïve, too.

1. How does the *i* in *naïve* sound: **ee** or **ay**? _____

2. What does *naïve* mean?   a. full of fun   b. soft and squishy   c. lacking in wisdom

3. The author uses very short sentences to emphasize certain ideas. List them. _____

_____

4. How does the author feel about the parents who let their kids play King of the Mountain?

_____

Day #3

A youthful attacker, missing his target, slid over a snow mound and skidded into the path of a fast-approaching snowplow. Only because a fellow player grabbed him by the collar and yanked him into a ditch was a catastrophe avoided. The near-victim was so shaken that he remained in bed for a week.

1. Do you pronounce the *e* in *catastrophe*?_____

2. What is the suffix in *youthful*? What does *youthful* mean? _____

3. If you read sentence 1 out loud, how would you read it to reflect the action it describes?
   a. lazily   b. quickly   c. really loudly

4. Do the descriptions of the game make you want to play it or want to avoid it? Explain.

_____

Day #4

Save the Day

Tate raced toward the baseball diamond. He greeted his teammates, jumping up and down. "Are you ready to win the championship?" he asked excitedly.

His two best friends, Jeffrey and Alyssa, smiled at his excitement. "It looks like our star batter is ready," Jeffrey said. Jeffrey didn't want to admit that he was pretty nervous. Lately, he'd been in a slump. His average had declined late in the season. He hoped he could pull it back up today when it counted most.

Alyssa was calm, as usual. She never seemed to get butterflies in her stomach, even under pressure. She was the team's pitcher and had a mean fastball.

The players warmed up and took the field. The game was a close one, but Tate and his team were victorious in the end. Afterward, the three buddies went to a nearby ice-cream shop to celebrate.

"Great job today, Alyssa!" Tate complimented his friend. "You kept your cool even when we were behind 2 to 0."

"Thanks," Alyssa said modestly. She licked her black raspberry cone neatly. Not a drip escaped off the cone.

"You were pretty great yourself," Jeffrey said to Tate. "I jumped off the bench, almost knocking it over, when you hit that ball over the fence in the fifth inning!" The two boys gave each other high fives. In their enthusiasm, the boys knocked Tate's ice cream off its cone.

"Oh, no," Tate said, disappointedly.

"Sorry, Tate," Jeffrey said. But Jeffrey couldn't stop smiling. He was in too good a mood. He'd hit the winning run today, and he felt great. He hadn't let his team down. Now, he wouldn't let his friend down.

"I have some money left," he said to Tate. "Let's go back up to the counter so I can save the day again!"

1. Find a word that has a *u* with an **oo** sound. _____

2. What is a synonym for *celebrate* as it is used here: **party** or **observe**?

3. Compare how each kid feels before the game. _____

   _____

4. The author tells you that Alyssa doesn't get too nervous. What actions of hers tell you that she doesn't get too excited either? _____

   _____

5. Which kid is a bit of a klutz? How do you know? _____

   _____

The Sydney Opera House

The Sydney Opera House is world-famous. It has an unusual design. It is one of the most unusual buildings in the world. The Opera House is Sydney's most famous landmark. It's located in Sydney Harbor.

1. What clues does the title give you?_____

2. Does the first paragraph tell you where Sydney is? _____

3. Do you think the opera house is near water?_____

4. What details from the paragraph helped you answer #3? _____
   _____

Day #1

Danish architect Jørn Utson designed the Sydney Opera House. He won a contest for his design. Work began in 1959 and was completed in 1973. The estimate for the Sydney Opera House was $7 million (Australian). However, the final cost was $102 million.

1. Does this paragraph give you a clue about where Sydney is? If so, where?
   _____

2. How long did it take to build the Sydney Opera House? _____

3. How much over budget was the building?_____

4. Was the cost estimate very accurate?_____

Day #2

Utson wanted the roof to look like sails on a giant sailing ship. Some people think the roof looks like huge seashells. The roof is made of ten gigantic arched concrete shell shapes. The shells have ribs that curve inward. Concrete joins the ribs where they meet. One of the biggest cranes in the world lifted the concrete roof pieces into place. Working on the building was dangerous because of the roof.

1. Does the Sydney Opera House look like Utson wanted it to? _____

2. What clues helped you answer #1?_____

3. How does the author describe the shape: **sails** or **shells**? _____

4. What do you think the danger was with the roof? _____

Day #3

The Opera House contains one hall for operas. The symphony orchestra plays concerts in another hall. A third hall is for plays. A fourth is for chamber music. The fifth is for exhibitions.

1. What fraction of halls are used for music? _____

2. What kinds of music do symphony orchestras and chamber music groups play?

   a. hip-hop   b. classical   c. contemporary country

3. Which, if any, of the activities that take place in the Sydney Opera House would you enjoy? _____

4. What kind of music or other event do you think they should have at the opera house?
   _____

Day #4

1. Have you ever seen a lighthouse before?

_____

Lighthouses

Imagine you're trying to get home. A storm has been raging for hours. The sea has been tossing your small sailing craft up and down, and you're not sure where you are. Suddenly in the distance, you see a faint light. You know you're safe and almost home.

2. What kind of writing does paragraph one seem like: **fiction** or **nonfiction**?

_____

Lighthouses were built to guide ships into coastal waters. They were built at dangerous points on a coastline, usually near reefs or at entrances to harbors. The earliest known lighthouse was built in Egypt. It was called Pharos. Pharos was completed about 280 B.C.

3. What is the cause that leads to a lighthouse being built?

_____

Boston Light was built in 1716. It was the first lighthouse in the New World. Within years, lighthouses were built in Canada and in South Carolina. By the time the Declaration of Independence was signed in 1776, there were 12 lighthouses, most in New England. In 1800, the U.S. had 16, and by 1812, there were about 49 lighthouses. The first West Coast lighthouses were completed in 1854 and 1855 in California.

4. How many years passed between the first lighthouse and the first lighthouse in the New World? (Remember that the first one was in B.C., not A.D.)

_____

5. About how many times more lighthouses were there in 1812 than there were in 1776? _____

A Delicious Dinner

Molly is Chinese American. Her family members gather together and serve a traditional Chinese meal once a week. Molly invited her friend Amy to join them for it this week.

1. Which word has two *e*'s—one that is pronounced and the other that is not? _____

2. What does *traditional* mean?

   a. information and customs handed down from one generation to another
   b. really old-fashioned
   c. boring

3. What is the "it" in "join them for it this week"? _____

4. Is Molly from China? _____

Molly's family was busy preparing for dinner when Amy arrived. Molly directed Amy through the living room to the kitchen, which was filled with many good smells. "You can help me set the table," Molly told her friend. They gave each person a pair of chopsticks, a soup bowl, a soup spoon, and a rice bowl on a saucer.

1. Which word rhymes with *busy*: **Susy** or **dizzy**? _____

2. Which word is a better replacement for *good smells*: **aroma** or **odor**? _____

3. How many individual items do the girls put at each place? _____

4. How many chopsticks does each person get? _____

The two girls went into the kitchen. Molly's father was slicing and chopping vegetables. He threw the vegetables into a large cooking pan coated with hot oil. "That's a wok," Molly said. Amy watched the vegetables sizzle.

1. Fill the blanks with homophones. After we cook dinner in the _____, we can go for a _____.

2. What is a wok? _____

3. Find an example of onomatopoeia. _____

4. How do you think is Amy used to eating? _____

Molly's mother scooped different foods onto big plates. She asked the girls to carry the food-filled plates out to the table. Amy carried steamed rice. It was one of the few dishes she recognized. There were meat-filled bundles called wontons, steamed noodles, stir-fried beef, sweet-and-sour chicken, and pork spareribs. The nutritious food was seasoned with herbs, spices, and sauces.

1. What sound does the *tious* in *nutritious* make: **teeus** or **shus**? _____

2. What does *nutritious* mean? _____

3. Circle the only thing Amy was familiar with before the dinner.
   wok   chopsticks   rice   wontons

4. Do you think Amy was upset about being asked to help? _____

Assessment

A Delicious Dinner (continued)

Once everyone was at the table, they quickly began eating. Their chopsticks moved quickly and made small clicking noises as they grabbed the food.

Amy was a little nervous about eating with chopsticks. Molly gave her instructions on how to hold and pinch with the chopsticks.

Amy finally managed to pick up a piece of chicken in her chopsticks. Suddenly, her fingers slipped, and the chicken flew across the table. It landed in Molly's soup with a splash. Everyone smiled. Molly's grandmother, who came every week to the family meal, patted Amy on the arm.

"We keep these on hand for emergencies," Molly's father said kindly. He brought out a fork and knife. He handed them to Amy.

Amy was relieved. She ate the rest of her dinner easily. It was delicious!

At the end of the meal, everyone was given a fortune cookie. Amy broke hers open and read it. "If you practice hard, you will learn many things." Amy laughed and said, "If you let me take home a pair of chopsticks, my fortune may come true!"

1. Find a compound word. _____

2. What sense of *fortune* is used here: **lots of money** or **a prediction**? _____
_____

3. Find two examples of onomatopoeia. _____
_____

4. What did Molly's family do to make Amy feel comfortable after the chopstick incident? _____
_____

5. Write a different ending for the story, starting after the chopstick incident.
_____
_____
_____

The World Series

Baseball is an important part of American culture and history. The World Series is the most exciting and important sporting event of the year because it names the national champion in America's favorite pastime.

1. Does the title tell you anything specific about the World Series? _____
2. Underline the part of sentence 2 that is the author's opinion.
3. Circle the part of sentence 2 that is fact.
4. How does the author feel about baseball? _____
   _____

Day #1

In spite of what the title says, the World Series is actually not a championship open to the world. The World Series matches the American League champion team against the National League champion team. The first team to win four games out of seven wins the World Series.

1. Is the World Series an accurate name for this sporting event? Why or why not?
   _____
2. Do you think the World Series needs a new name that is more accurate? _____
3. How do the two teams end up in the World Series? _____
4. Is the World Series won in the best of seven or the best of five games? _____

Day #2

The World Series was first played in 1903. The American League champions, the Boston Pilgrims, played the National League champions, the Pittsburgh Pirates. The Boston Pilgrims, now named the Boston Red Sox, won this first World Series. Boston won a few more times, but the last time for many decades was in 1918. They didn't win the World Series again until 2004.

1. Who won the first World Series? _____
2. What are the Boston Pilgrims now? _____
3. How many years passed between Red Sox titles? _____
4. About how many decades is your answer to #3? _____

Day #3

Making it to the World Series takes hard work and a lot of talent. Most teams play over 150 games between April and October each year. Many great baseball players, such as Babe Ruth, Jackie Robinson, Joe Di Maggio and Lou Gehrig, have played in the World Series.

1. Have you heard of any of those "great baseball players"? If so, circle them.
2. If the headline "World Series Deemed Unnecessary" appeared in a local paper, how might the author of this story respond? _____
3. What other articles would you expect this author to write? _____
4. Think of a new name for the World Series. (It can't be American Series or National Series.) _____

Day #4

1. Have you ever heard of Jackie Robinson? Does the title give you any clues about who Robinson is?

_____

Jackie Robinson

As a young boy, Jackie joined the neighborhood Pepper Street gang and started stealing and throwing dirt at cars. A neighbor told Jackie that he would hurt his mother if she knew he was getting into trouble. The neighbor also told him that he would be showing more bravery if he didn't do what the gang wanted him to do. Jackie listened. It was then that he decided to become active in sports.

2. What important choice did Jackie make? _____

_____

In 1945, Jackie played shortstop for the Kansas City Monarchs, a team in the Negro League. Professional baseball was still segregated. It was at this time that the president of the Brooklyn Dodgers, Branch Rickey, recognized Jackie's talent in baseball.

Branch Rickey was determined to make Jackie Robinson the first African-American player in major league baseball. Jackie started playing with the Dodgers' farm club. Rickey advised Jackie not to fight back when people were unkind to him.

In 1947, Jackie started playing professional baseball for the Brooklyn Dodgers. At first, his teammates didn't like playing with him. However, when other teams taunted Jackie, his teammates came to his defense. Because of his great performance at second base and his outstanding batting average, he was selected as Rookie of the Year. In 1949, he was named the Most Valuable Player in the National League. One of his greatest thrills was when he helped the Dodgers win the 1955 World Series.

Jackie Robinson paved the hard path for African-American men to play in the major leagues. In 1962, he was inducted into baseball's Hall of Fame. Ten years later, in Stamford, Connecticut, Jackie Robinson died at the age of 53.

3. What does the article tell you was historic about Jackie Robinson?

_____

4. What does it mean that baseball was still segregated in 1945? _____

_____

5. What advice did Branch Rickey give Jackie? _____

_____

Hooray for Hair

Have you ever considered the many characteristics of your hair? While your hair may improve your appearance, it also has important functions.

1. Does the *pear* in *appearance* sound more like **peer** or **pear**?_____

2. What is the opposite of *improve*?_____

3. What does the title tell you about how the author feels about hair?_____
_____

4. Do you think the rest of this article will deal with solutions for bad hair days or cool information about hair?_____

Hair protects the body. It acts as a cushion protecting the head from bumps and bruises. Hair can be a shield from the hot summer sun and keep the head warm on chilly winter days. Inside the nose and ears, tiny hairs deter dirt, dust, and insects from entering the body. Eyebrows are patches of hair that trap perspiration before it is able to reach the eyes. Eyelashes prevent dirt and dust from infecting the eyes.

1. Which syllable do you emphasize when you say *deter*? _____

2. List all the words that mean *keep away*. _____

3. What is another, more common word for perspiration?_____

4. What hair protects our eyes?_____

Each hair on the body grows from a root beneath the skin. This root forms a tiny tube called a follicle. As new hair cells grow from the root, the old cells are pushed up, and since they are no longer being fed, they soon die. The dead cells harden, forming a stack on top of a root, referred to as a hair shaft. Only the follicle and the root remain alive, so it doesn't hurt to cut hair.

1. What syllable do you emphasize when you say *follicle*? _____

2. What is a follicle? _____

3. What is a hair shaft made of? _____

4. What are the three parts of each hair? _____

Have you ever wished for a different type of hair? Maybe you would like straighter hair, or perhaps you wish your hair had more curl. The shape of the hair shaft, as seen in a cross section under a microscope, determines the degree of curliness or straightness. Straight hairs are round in structure. The flatter the hair shaft, the curlier the hair will be. You cannot change your hair follicles, but hair straighteners and permanents can alter the appearance of hair temporarily.

1. Which word has the most syllables? How many syllables?_____

2. Which two words in this paragraph are synonyms for *modify*?_____

3. What shape is your hair shaft?_____

4. What was the author's purpose in writing this article?_____

Assessment

The Right Choice

Throughout history, people have been faced with critical choices. Sometimes, people's choices have made the world a better place for everyone. Sometimes, they have made the world a better place only for themselves. It all comes down to choices.

The period of slavery in this country was a time of crucial choices. While some bound slaves in chains, others did all they could to oppose slavery. William Still, a free black man in Philadelphia, jeopardized his own safety and freedom to get others through the Underground Railroad route.

Despite the bounty on the head of Harriet Tubman, she chose to keep helping others. She dressed up as a man and continued to help others escape. Harriet's friend, Thomas Garrett, a white businessman, was fined $5,400 (a huge amount in the 1800s) and arrested for his part in the Underground Railroad. Knowing he was doing the right thing, Thomas nevertheless continued his Underground Railroad work.

Less than 100 years later, society was once again faced with pivotal choices. There were those who chose to do the work of the Nazis and kill and imprison innocent Jews. Then there was Miep Gies, the Dutch woman who helped hide Anne Frank's Jewish family for 25 months. There was Oskar Schindler, a German businessman. He saved more than 1,000 Polish Jews by having them work in his "factory." The factory was actually a safe haven for the Jews. There were many more "Oskars" and "Mieps" during this horrible period.

1. Does the first syllable of *jeopardized* sound more like the first syllable of **geography** or **Jennifer**? _____

2. What does *jeopardized* mean? _____

3. If the author read this piece out loud, how do you think he or she would read it: **passionately** or **without much expression**? _____

4. What is the right choice, according to the author? _____

   _____

5. What is the author's purpose in writing this? Circle all that apply.

   a. to inform you about people who have made the right choice

   b. to make you feel depressed about the state of the world

   c. to encourage you to make the right choices

   d. to persuade you to travel around the world seeking out injustice

Name _____

Week #30

Antarctica and the Sahara

Antarctica is the continent surrounding the South Pole. It contains 90 percent of the world's ice. Antarctica is the coldest and most desolate region on Earth. It covers 5,400,000 square miles. Much of the land is buried under snow and ice one mile thick. Winter temperatures reach -100°F in the interior of the continent. On the coast, temperatures fall below -40°F.

1. What clues does the title give you about what the author will be doing in this article?
   _____

2. What does *desolate* mean?_____

3. What is the difference between the highest and lowest temperatures? _____

4. Do you think any native people live on Antarctica? _____

Day #1

Stretching almost 3,000 miles across North Africa, the Sahara Desert is an incredible natural wonder of sand, rock, and gravel. The Sahara covers over 3,500,000 square miles, which makes it by far the largest desert on Earth. Its sandy surface may reach a temperature of 170°F. The cloudless skies allow the daytime air temperature to reach 100°F. At night, the temperature often drops 40 to 50 degrees.

1. Is the Sahara Desert a continent? _____

2. What is the difference between the surface temperature of the sand and the daytime air temperature? _____

3. Which is larger: **Antarctica** or the **Sahara Desert**?_____

4. What is the difference between the winter temperature of the interior of Antarctica and the daytime air temperature of the Sahara? (One is below 0 and the other is above 0.) _____

Day #2

The interior of Antarctica is a frozen, lifeless region. The only animal life in Antarctica is found on the coastline or in the sea. Penguins, seals, whales, and other fish and birds live in or close to the coastal waters. These animals live on food from the sea.

1. What lives on Antarctica? Does the list include people?_____

2. Do any plants grow in Antarctica? _____

3. What synonym for *desolate* appears in this paragraph? _____

4. What color(s) do you imagine when you think of the landscape of Antarctica?
   _____

Day #3

The Sahara's only vegetation is found near wells, springs, or streams. These fertile areas are called oases. Throughout the desert are many dry streambeds, called wadis. During a rare rain, they temporarily fill up with water. The Sahara supports some animal life, too—camels, lizards, and the addax, a desert antelope.

1. What kinds of things are able to live and grow in the Sahara Desert? _____

2. What colors do you imagine when you think of the landscape of the Sahara Desert?
   _____

3. Make a comparison chart for Antarctica and the Sahara Desert. Include these categories: size, what it's made of, warmest air temperature, coldest air temperature, vegetation, animals.

4. Which place would you rather visit? Explain. _____

Day #4

Published by Frank Schaffer Publications. Copyright protected. 0-7682-3215-5 *Read 4 Today*

Assessment

1. What clues does the title tell you about the topic of this selection?

_____

The Exchange Student

Lorraine and her parents and three brothers have decided to host an exchange student for a year. They had to supply lots of information about themselves so they could be matched to a student with interests similar to theirs.

2. What does the above paragraph tell you about the members of Lorraine's family? _____

The family has to decide between two students. Help them decide by reading the information about the two students below.

Corinne

    loves cats, dogs, rabbits
    loves hiking, camping, fishing
    loves small children
    has two brothers and one sister
    likes to cook and try new foods
    doesn't like to read or study
    will share a room
    wants to travel all over the U.S.

3. Check all that apply.
   If Lorraine's family chooses Corinne, they probably—
   A. do a lot of outdoor activities.
   B. watch a lot of TV
   C. have animals.
   D. want to travel.

Bruno

    loves reading and writing
    allergic to animals
    an only child
    doesn't like small children
    likes to play video games, draw, play chess
    doesn't like to cook
    won't share a room
    wants to know well the family he stays with

4. Check all that apply.
   If Lorraine's family chooses Bruno, they probably—
   A. have no pets.
   B. have a spare bedroom.
   C. do a lot of outdoor activities.
   D. don't have small children.

5. Compare your answers to #3 and #4 with what you know about Lorraine's family. If you were Lorraine and her family, whom would you choose? Why?

_____

_____

"Hello. My name is Ansal Khamba. I am twelve years old and attend a school in the city of Calcutta, India." My mother says I should tell you something about our country of Bharat. That is the official name of India. It would be difficult to tell you briefly about our country. It is very old and has at least 5,000 years of recorded history. Perhaps I will tell you about some of our beautiful sights instead.

1. Write out 5,000. _____

2. What other word could you use instead of *perhaps*? _____

3. Does the author sound very excited to tell you about his country? _____

4. What clues from the paragraph helped you answer #3?_____
   _____

Day #1

My favorite place is the Taj Mahal. This magnificent structure is really a mausoleum, a building that houses the bodies of the dead. An emperor named Shah Jahan ordered this building be created to honor his dead wife, Mumtaz Mahal. Twenty thousand workers toiled twenty years to build this memorial. Inside is an ornate burial chamber where the emperor and his wife are now buried together.

1. Which word has a silent first letter? _____

2. What other word could you use instead of *toiled*? _____

3. Underline a sentence that expresses an opinion.

4. Circle a sentence that contains a fact.

Day #2

When I was eight years old, my mother took me on a trip to the Bandhavgarh National Park. The many birds of the park are beautiful. I loved the blues and greens of the peacock and the tinge of pink on the rosy pastor. Still, the park is most famous for the care and protection it offers to tigers.

1. Fill in the blanks with a homograph that appears in the paragraph.
   My _____ keeps a rosy _____ in his office at church.

2. What does *tinge* tell you about the kind of pink on the rosy pastor: **light blush** or
   deep stain? _____

3. Underline a sentence that expresses an opinion.

4. Circle a sentence that contains a fact.

Day #3

Two years ago, my father and mother took me to the Thar Desert. What a harsh place! I cannot imagine anyone living in a land like that. Yet, we saw ancient temples and palaces. We traveled by riding on camels. My camel, whose translated name meant "Stubborn and Foolish," was slow, single-minded, and mean. He spit on people, especially on Kogi, our guide's assistant.

1. List all the words that contain the **sh** sound. _____

2. What word in the second-last sentence is a synonym for *single-minded*? _____

3. Underline a sentence that expresses an opinion.

4. What evidence does Ansal give you to prove that his description of his camel is fact, not opinion? _____

Day #4

Flower Power

Jack's family loves flowers. They love planting them, and they enjoy going to flower shows. Jack isn't that crazy about flowers, but he did enjoy the flower show at the Dukwilma Fairgrounds.

There were hundreds of different kinds of flowers from all over the world at the show. Jack learned a lot while he was there. He didn't know that flowers were judged on their shape, color, and fragrance. He did know, however, that people use flowers to express their deepest feelings. His dad sent his mother flowers expressing his love quite often. Jack was also surprised to learn that certain flowers have religious significance. For instance, the white Easter lily stands for purity, and Buddhists and Hindus regard the lotus as sacred.

Jack found it interesting that originally all flowers were wild flowers. People have since learned to cultivate a variety of flowers. Jack saw beautiful flowers such as sunflowers, violets, daffodils, lilacs, and lilies among many others at the show. His favorite flowers, however, were the gorgeous roses.

1. The beginning sounds of *purity* sound more like **sure** or **pure**? _____

2. Fill in the blank with a synonym of *stands for*. The Easter lily is a _____ of purity.

3. Check all that apply. Jack's dad sends his mother flowers

   _____ to express his feelings.
   _____ for no reason.
   _____ a lot.
   _____ for her birthday.

4. Underline a sentence in the last paragraph that expresses an opinion.

5. Circle a sentence in the last paragraph that contains a fact.

Lazy Time

Sally and Ned are swaying slowly in the family swing.

1. What does the title tell us about the story?_____

2. What information does the opening sentence add? _____

3. Is there an image in the first sentence that supports or illustrates the title?

   _____

4. If so, what is it and how does it illustrate the title? _____

   _____

The air is crisp. Sally puts her arm around Ned and snuggles into his shaggy body. Ned's tongue licks Sally's hand that lies on her blue-jeaned leg. They watch a sluggish ladybug crawl underneath a pile of old, brown leaves. One red leaf drifts down to the top of the ladybug's leaf pile.

1. What time of year is it?_____

2. What clues helped you answer #1?_____

3. What or who do you think Ned is? _____

4. What clues helped you answer #3?_____

Ned's graying ears prick up as a southbound V of geese honks goodbye. The sky slowly turns from blue, to pink, to purple, to black.

The first star shines as Sally's mom calls her in to eat. Sally gives a last push as she slides out of the swing. She walks to the back door of the house. Ned leaps down.

1. What sounds can you hear in this selection? _____

2. Is Ned a puppy or an older dog?_____

3. What clues helped you answer #2?_____

4. How do you think Sally feels?_____

Ned barks once at a rabbit, and then chases after Sally. She smiles and rubs Ned's head as they walk into the warm house together.

1. What meal is Sally about to eat? _____

2. Did the title set up the story well?_____

3. List the words in all the selections that give a picture of laziness. _____

   _____

4. What other title would work?_____

Assessment

1. This is a table of contents for a book. What does a table of contents tell you?

    _____

A Year in My Life

CONTENTS

2. What time of year is it in chapters 2 and 3? _____

3. What season is it in chapters 7–9? _____

4. Do you think chapter 13 is about the harvest festival of Thanksgiving or about the author harvesting food from a garden? What clues helped you answer that question?_____

    _____

5. Is the book arranged thematically (by theme) or chronologically (by time)?

    _____

Twelve Toes

They call me a three-toed sloth, but everyone definitely knows
When you count them all up, I have 12 gorgeous toes.

1. Is *sloth* pronounced more like **both** or **broth**? _____

2. What word could you use instead of *count*: **add** or **multiply**? _____

3. From whose point of view is this piece written? _____

4. What genre of writing is this? _____

I'm passionate about a climate that's tropical and warm,
I wouldn't live anywhere that would have a snowstorm.
I require splendid, tropical rain forests in order to survive,
For, if it weren't for them, I most certainly wouldn't be alive.
You can find me in the Americas—either South or Central—
From Argentina and Guatemala to the Honduras and even Brazil.

1. Are the vowel sounds in *climate* the same as the vowel sounds in **primate**? _____

2. What does *survive* mean? _____

3. Rewrite "I'm passionate about a climate that's tropical and warm" in your own words.

4. Would the three-toed sloth live in a forest in Missouri? _____

My teeth grow constantly, every second of
   the hour, every minute that ticks by,

Thank goodness I grind them when I chew
   my food, or else they'd reach to the sky!

I'm a downright clever mammal,
   with a brownish green skin

That protects me from my enemies
   by helping me to blend in.

I'm a nocturnal animal,
   so I snooze during the day,

I feast only on scrumptious plants,
   and I like it that way.

1. Find a compound word. _____

2. What other word could you use instead of *scrumptious*? _____

3. What is the rhyme scheme of this poem?
   a. aa bb cc dd
   b. abab cdcd
   c. free verse

4. Is the three-toed sloth a carnivore or an herbivore? What clues helped you answer that question? _____

You humans might enjoy living in a bustling, noisy city or a quaint, small town,
But for me, the best place to be is a tropical rain forest tree, hanging upside down!

1. Which word in this last stanza has a silent letter in the middle? _____

2. What does *bustling* mean? _____

3. Why did the author write this poem?
   a. to entertain you with silly sloth talk
   b. to inform you about the sloth's habitat and habits
   c. to persuade you to have a sloth for a pet

4. What is the sloth's favorite position? _____

A Doomed Romance

You are my love, my love you are.
I worship you from afar;
I through the branches spy you.

You, Sir, are a climbing thug.
I do not like your fuzzy mug.
Away from me, please take you!

Oh, grant me peace, my love, my dove.
Climb to my home so far above
This place you call your warren.

I like my home in sheltered hollow
Where fox and weasel may not follow.
Please go away, tree rodent!

I love your ears, so soft and tall.
I love your nose, so pink and small.
I must make you my own bride!

I will not climb, I cannot eat
The acorns that you call a treat.
Now shimmy up that oak; hide!

Now I hide up in my bower.
Lonesome still, I shake and cower.
Sadness overtakes me.

I must stay on the lovely ground
With carrots crisp and cabbage round.
I long for gardens, not trees.

1. Find an example of alliteration._____

2. What other word could you use instead of *shimmy* in stanza 6? _____

3. What is the rhyme scheme in this poem?
   a. a,b,a / c,b,c
   b. a,b,b / c,b,b
   c. a,a,b / c,c,b

4. Who are the two speakers in this ballad? Identify them and write one adjective to describe the tone of each voice.

   a. _____

   b. _____

5. What do you think the theme of this poem is? Write it in one phrase or sentence._____

The Incredible George Washington Carver

George Washington Carver was born in 1861. His parents were slaves. They lived on a plantation in Missouri.

1. What does the title tell you about the subject of this article?_____
   _____

2. What opinion word is in the title? _____

3. Was George born into a privileged situation? _____

4. Who do you think was he named after? _____

Day #1

George Washington Carver was often sick as a child. He couldn't help around the plantation. He liked to spend time in the woods. There he found flowers and plants. He made a collection of them. George taught himself to read. He was very independent. He left the plantation to live on his own. He was ten years old.

1. What was the effect of George's childhood illnesses? _____

2. What did George do instead of work on the plantation? _____

3. What is a surprising fact in the end of the paragraph?_____

4. Can you imagine leaving home and living on your own in the next year or so?
   _____

Day #2

George wanted to go to a college. The college refused to admit him because he was black. George Washington Carver finally went to college. He was an excellent student. He took botany and chemistry classes. After he graduated, he taught classes at a college in Iowa. He was also director of a greenhouse.

1. Does George give up easily?_____

2. What clues helped you answer #1?_____

3. What kind of classes are botany and chemistry: **literature** or **science**?_____

4. What clues tell you whether Carver was a hard worker?_____
   _____

Day #3

George Washington Carver was a scientist. He discovered more than three hundred uses for the peanut plant. Among his discoveries were shampoo, car grease, soap, rubber, wood filler, paint, and shoe polish. His research helped farmers.

1. What was the effect of George's research? _____

2. What character traits did George have? _____

3. What was the effect of George's plant collecting when he was a boy?
   _____

4. Do you agree with the author's title—is George Washington Carver Incredible? Why or why not? _____

Day #4

Assessment

1. What does the title tell us about the subject of this article?

_____

A Simple Machine

Most people welcome a new invention that makes life easier, but when the cotton gin arrived in 1793, it was the slaves' worst nightmare.

2. After reading the first paragraph, predict what the rest of the article will prove. _____

At that time, Southerners weren't making as much money as they wanted from their crops, especially cotton. One kind of cotton was simple to de-seed, but it thrived only near water. Another type was hard to de-seed, but it grew anywhere inland.

Enter Eli Whitney, a Yale graduate who moved to Georgia. Eli sized up the cotton situation. Within a short time, this brilliant young man invented the cotton gin. The gin detached the seeds from the soft cottony fibers. The sturdy, inland cotton could quickly be de-seeded. The machine was unbelievably simple and used wires, a drum, and a brush.

3. What important step in making cotton did the cotton gin simplify?

_____

Growing cotton could now make a lot of money for the plantation owners. They stopped grumbling and began exporting cotton and importing slaves. Who else could work the fields? Who else could pick the large amounts of cotton that were fed into the super machine?

Between 1790 and 1808 (when it became illegal), 80,000 Africans were shipped to the South. The cotton gin helped the South produce 75 percent of the cotton the world used. The Southerners wanted an important crop to export, and now they had one. In 1860, the South produced around 5 million bales of cotton. Sadly, about one third of the people in the South were slaves that same year.

All Eli Whitney wanted was to make life easier. Instead, life for thousands became so much harder.

4. What is the author's opinion of Eli Whitney? _____

_____

5. What is the author's opinion of Eli Whitney's invention? _____

_____

Where, Oh Where?

I'm a very forgetful person, so it didn't surprise any of my friends when I shouted, "I've lost my science report!"

1. Which part of *forgetful* is the root and which part is the suffix?_____

2. What does *forgetful* mean? _____

3. If you were reading this story out loud, describe how you'd read, "I've lost my science report!"

   _____

4. Which point of view is this written from?
   a. first person   b. second person   c. third person

Paul, Ansil, and Lena all gave suggestions as to possible locations of the report, but one by one, they were eliminated. I hadn't stopped at my locker, the girls' gym, the computer lab, or the cafeteria. I even called home, after waiting in line to use the pay phone in the main courtyard.

1. Which **gg** or **g** sounds more like the **gg** in *suggestions*: **giggle** or **gingerbread**? _____

2. What does *eliminated* mean in this paragraph? _____

3. The author has good friends because they tried to help the author. What would bad friends have done in this situation?_____

4. Does this paragraph give you any clues whether the author is a boy or a girl? If so, what is that clue? _____

Mom was particularly upset, especially since she'd been the one driving me all over town while I was doing research and buying just the right shade of light blue printer paper. She had also done me the huge favor of typing the ten-page report.

"Tara! How could you possibly misplace something so important? Did you check your backpack? Your locker?" Then she repeated my friends' suggestions.

1. Break down the word *misplace* into its syllables. _____

2. Which word in this selection is a synonym for *lose*?_____

3. If you read this story out loud, how would you read the mother's words. _____

   _____

4. What new information do you learn about the author? _____

Study hall was over. I had one period left before science, and I was pretty nervous. I wanted to earn another A in science. It would look so great on my report card—straight A's across the sheet. But this report was a major part of our final grade in Mrs. Hernandez's class. As I sat in geography, mentally retracing my steps and combing my memory for ideas on the report's location, I had a great idea.

1. Which word has two of the same consonant, one in the beginning and one in the middle of the word, but each consonant is pronounced differently? _____

2. The words that *geography* came from are *geo*, which means "earth," and *graphein*, which means "to write." So what does the word *geography* mean? _____

3. Do you think Tara will remember anything the teacher said in her geography class? _____

4. How well does Tara normally do in school? How do you know? _____

Where, Oh Where? (continued)

I would simply tell Mrs. Hernandez that I had decided to do further research because I was so excited about the subject and that I hadn't finished typing it. I would tell her that my mother had offered to finish typing it but had broken her finger. I would just have to come up with some incredible and airtight excuse.

As I slowly wandered toward the science lab, silently rehearsing my excuses, I began to feel guilty. Could I actually look my favorite teacher in the eye and lie about my report? How would I feel then? Maybe worse than I felt when I realized that it was missing.

I tossed my backpack over my shoulder, straightened my back, and walked into the room. Taking a deep breath, I knew what I had to do—I would tell the truth.

I walked up to Mrs. Hernandez's desk to speak with her. As she looked up from the thick stack of papers in front of her, she lightly tapped the top report, a report typed on baby blue paper in a transparent folder.

"Oh, Tara!" said Mrs. Hernandez, "I'm always glad when one or two students hand in these larger reports early. I can really take my time reading them then. Your research on whale migration is incredible. Would you mind sharing with the class?"

I thought I would fall over! How in the world had this happened? All this worrying and waiting!

1. Is the **ui** sound in *guilty* more like the **ui** sound in **suite** or **build**?_____

2. What does *transparent* mean? _____

3. If you were reading this story out loud, what facial expression would you use for Tara's response to her teacher's words? _____
   _____

4. Does the teacher sound pleased with Tara's report? How do you know?
   _____
   _____

5. What did it turn out that Tara forgot? _____
   _____

Television

The invention of the television changed the world in many important ways. Television gave people the opportunity to see and hear about people, places, and events around the world. Over 98 percent of all U.S. homes have a television. Television is now an important form of communication, allowing people instant access to current events.

1. What clues does the title give you about the topic of this article?_____

2. Does the first paragraph narrow down the topic? If so, how? _____

3. The author uses *important* twice. Change one of those sentences, using a synonym for *important*._____

4. What is the topic sentence of this paragraph? _____

Television does not have just one inventor. In the 1800s, an Italian inventor named Marconi set the stage when he discovered how to send signals through the air as electromagnetic waves. His invention was the radio. In the early 1900s, a young American named Philo Farnsworth had an idea to send pictures as well as sound through the air. This led to the invention of the electronic television camera.

1. What invention set the stage for the invention of TV?_____

2. About how many years passed between that invention and the next step? _____

3. What was the next step?_____

4. About how many years have passed between that invention and now?_____

About the same time, an American scientist named Vladimir Zworykin invented the iconoscope and the kinescope. The iconoscope was a television camera. The kinescope was a picture tube to receive and show the picture. In 1929, Zworykin made the first television system.

1. What were the next steps in the invention of television? _____

2. Inventors from which country were involved in the most steps? _____

3. Do you know anyone who was alive in 1929? _____

4. Do you think Farnsworth or Zworykin made a lot of money from their invention of the television?_____

How does a television work? First, light and sound waves are changed into electronic signals by cameras and microphones. Next, these electronic signals are passed through the air to be received by individual television sets. Last, the television set unscrambles the signals.

1. How many steps are there to get to the picture you see on your TV?_____

2. What are those steps? _____

3. Which kind of wave does a camera change into an electronic signal?

    _____

4. What is the most important thing about television for you?_____

Day #1

Day #2

Day #3

Day #4

1. Have you ever heard of Philo Farnsworth?

_____

Philo Farnsworth and Television

What would you say if someone asked who had invented the transmission, or sending, of television images? If you do not know the answer, you are not alone. Most people do not know that this was an invention of Philo Farnsworth. This is probably because a large company took Farnsworth's idea.

2. Why have most people not heard of Philo Farnsworth? _____

_____

Farnsworth was born in a log cabin in 1906. When he was twelve, his family moved to a ranch. This put Farnsworth miles away from his school, and he rode his horse to get there.

Farnsworth was very interested in the electron and electricity. He asked one of his teachers to teach him outside of class and to let him sit in on a course for older students. The teacher agreed. He came up with the idea for sending television pictures when he was only fourteen.

3. What year did Farnsworth have the idea? _____

An article told of his invention when he was only twenty-two. How did it work? Moving images, or pictures, were broken into pinpoints of light. These pinpoints were changed into electrical impulses, or movements. Then the impulses were collected by the television set and changed back to light. People could see the images. A major magazine listed Farnsworth as one of the 100 greatest scientists and thinkers of the twentieth century.

4. What year did the article appear in? _____

5. Do you think Farnsworth made a lot of money from his invention of television? Explain your reasoning.

_____

_____

_____

Baby, It's Cold Outside!

Picture yourself as a geologist studying Earth's outer shell. You are at the end of Earth, occupying a research station on the coldest continent in the world. You are at a place where no people live permanently. You are on the continent of Antarctica.

1. List all the words with four syllables. _____

2. What does it mean to live somewhere permanently?_____

3. What is the purpose of the first paragraph? _____

   _____

4. Which continent is the coldest? _____

Day #1

You are not alone. There are about 40 permanent research stations on this icy mass. Scientists, medical researchers, and biologists are all here. They come from about thirty countries to learn more about this frigid area.

1. Is the *g* in *frigid* a hard **g** or a soft **g**? _____

2. List all the words in this paragraph that have to do with how cold Antarctica is.

   _____

3. What is the main idea of this paragraph?_____

4. If you are a researcher in Antarctica, is there a good chance you will meet other researchers who don't speak your language? How do you know? _____

   _____

Day #2

Antarctica, with all its beauty, is not an easy place to live. In December and January there are up to 20 hours of sunlight during the month. That means almost total darkness during the winter. That's when the temperature can plunge to -100°F (-38°C)! People who've been here for at least a year can sometimes feel and act like prisoners of war.

1. What are the root and the suffix of *darkness*? _____

2. What other word could you use instead of *plunge*? _____

3. Which fact about Antarctica from this paragraph do you find the most surprising?

   _____

4. What is the most amount of sun in Antarctica during the entire month of December or January? _____

Day #3

While the researchers are serious about their work, they have fun, too. In their free time, they play pool and video games and read good books from the station libraries. There are concerts and festivals celebrating the first and last days of sun. Feasts, plays, songs, and games take center court around June 22. What's the reason for all the celebration? Antarctica's winter is half over!

1. Does *pool* rhyme with **good book**? _____

2. What is an antonym for *delicious*? _____

3. The author forgot to add this sentence to the passage: "The knowledge they have gained through the research done here has helped the worlds of medicine, science, and conservation." In which paragraph would this sentence best fit? _____

   _____

4. What is happening in North America around June 22? _____

Day #4

0-7682-3215-5 *Read 4 Today*

Show Time

(1) This light show lasts about 15 to 40 minutes. It can happen again two or three hours later. The wind on an Antarctic day can whip around at 200 miles an hour (322 km/hr). It's nice to know this phenomenon is around to warm any hearts.

(2) Antarctica's Aurora Australis can be seen almost every night in the winter. Usually, auroras are shaped like curtains hanging in the sky or as streamers or curves of light. The colors range from red to violet but are mostly light green or pink.

(3) Four words are often used to describe Antarctica. They are *dry*, *frigid*, *windy*, and *remote*. Visitors here also have high praise for this icy wonderland, particularly when the Aurora Australis lights up the sky.

(4) An aurora is a burst of energy that appears in the sky. It all starts 50 to 100 miles (80–129 km) above Earth's surface. Protons and electrons are given off by the sun. These particles crash into gases in the Earth's magnetic field. Then, the atoms get electrified. This produces colored light. Because Antarctica is south of the equator, it is in the Southern Hemisphere. Auroras here are called Aurora Australis. Another name is the Southern Lights. Auroras north of the equator are called Aurora Borealis.

1. In which word is the vowel pair *au* pronounced the same as the *o* in the word? _____

2. What does *remote* mean: **far away** or **a channel-changing device**?

    _____

3. What is the main subject of this article? _____

4. What is the difference between the Aurora Australis and the Aurora Borealis?

    _____

    _____

5. The article is jumbled. Reread it carefully to figure out which paragraph opens the article, which ones follow, and which one ends it. First comes paragraph _____, then _____, then _____, and then _____.

Sollie, the Rock

I've lived on a lake for most of my life. I love water sports, especially water skiing. That's why I invited my best friend, Sollie, over to give it a try. Sollie had never been on skis before, but I knew Dad could help him learn.

1. What clues does the title give us about the story? _____

2. Is Sollie an actual rock? _____

3. Who is Sollie? _____

4. Does the first paragraph tell us what Sollie has to do with a rock? _____

Day #1

Water skiing is like flying. I thought it would be easy. Sollie is a seal, sleek and smooth in the water. I thought someone so agile would find skiing easy. It didn't dawn on me until the fourth try that Sollie is more like a rock than a bird.

1. Does Sollie quickly learn to water ski? _____

2. What clues from the paragraph helped you answer #1? _____

3. Predict why Sollie might be more like a rock than a bird when he learns how to water ski.

_____

4. Which sentence above uses a metaphor? (for example, Bobby is a mouse)

_____

Day #2

On his first try, Sollie let go of the tow rope when Dad hit the gas. He sank like the *Titanic*. On his second try, Sollie leaned into the skis, flipping head over heels like a gymnast falling off the balance beam.

1. What is the *Titanic*? _____

2. Do you know because of knowledge you already have or because you are making an inference? _____

3. Which sentence in the paragraph uses a simile? (for example, Bobby is *like* a mouse)

_____

4. How many metaphors are in the paragraph? _____

Day #3

On the third try, Sollie stood up. He teetered forward and then back, as if he were a rag doll. He held on to the rope after he lost both skis. He flopped about behind the boat like a giant carp until he finally let go. On the fourth try, Sollie straightened his back and flew around the lake behind the boat as if he were a professional skier.

1. Which is your favorite simile in the last paragraph? Why? _____

2. Make a chart of the different kinds of things the author compares Sollie with. Use these categories: animals, people, things.

3. Which category does the author use most often? _____

4. Look back up to the title. Is the title a metaphor or a simile? _____

Day #4

Name

1. Glance down at the selection. What kind of writing is this?

_____

Whitesox

Sanding the board,
My cat, Whitesox.

2. What is Whitesox? Why do you think it was given that name? _____

_____

Her tongue,
Like fine grains of sand
On paper,
Licking the wood.

3. What simile is in the above selection?_____

_____

She is an electric sander
Giving out a quiet purr.
Like a nail file,
Smoothing out the edges.

4. When the author compares Whitesox with an electric sander, is that a
   metaphor or a simile?_____

_____

5. Do you think a cat's tongue is rough or smooth? Why? _____

_____

The Black Death

Nothing could stop this dreadful monster. It ravaged powerful cities and swallowed up small villages. It didn't care who it harmed, striking innocent babies and children just as often as old men and women.

1. List the words that have a *c* with a soft **c** sound. _____

2. What does *ravaged* mean?
   a. destroyed   b. changed   c. redesigned

3. Do you think the author is talking about an actual monster in this paragraph? _____

4. Restate "swallowed up small villages" in your own words. _____

Sickened rats roaming China in the 1330s are said to have started the chaos. Hungry fleas bit the infected rodents and then bit humans. Sick people and infected fleas then traveled on trading ships. "It" arrived in Italy by 1347. That year, 75 million people lived in Europe, yet five years later, the population dwindled to 50 million people.

1. Is the *ch* in *chaos* pronounced more like the *ch* in **change** or **character**? _____

2. What does *dwindled* mean?
   a. grew   b. maintained   c. shrank

3. What is the main idea of this paragraph? _____

4. Does this paragraph tell you what "It" is yet? _____

This horrid monster that ruined Europe during the Late Middle Ages was called the Black Death. This fast-spreading disease was also called the bubonic plague. Black tumors, high fever, red eyes, and a furry tongue were some of its gruesome symptoms. Once infected, hardly anyone survived the plague. Death was almost certain within thirty-six wretched hours.

1. Find a word that starts with a silent letter. _____

2. What word could you use instead of *gruesome*? _____

3. Which symptom do you think is the most gruesome? _____

4. What are the two names of the monster? _____

The plague killed millions, but those who escaped it were also affected. People questioned the church. They challenged the nobility. A peasant revolt occurred in the late 1300s. This miserable blight finally vanished in the 1600s. It is no surprise that even today we still say, "Avoid it like the plague."

1. Is the *g* in *plague* pronounced with a hard **g** or a soft **g**? _____

2. What word in this paragraph is a synonym for *questioned*? _____

3. What effect of the Black Death does this paragraph talk about? _____

4. About how many years did the bubonic plague affect Europe? _____

Assessment

The White Death

Going snowshoeing anytime soon? Don't forget your inclinometer!

An inclinometer is a clever device that could save your life. It measures the angle of a mountain slope. Knowing that angle could help you outwit an avalanche. Most avalanches run when the slope slants between 30 and 45 degrees. Imagine a capital L with a line extending to the right from the corner, equally dividing the L into two spaces. This line will give you an idea of what a 45-degree angle looks like. But these snow slides can happen no matter what the steepness of a mountain is. For instance, a mountain full of wet snow and a 25-degree angle could run.

However, the steepness of a mountain slope is only one cause of this White Death. Another cause is slope orientation. This means the direction the slope faces. Those slopes that face northeast, east, and north run the most risk. Other factors that can spark an avalanche include the terrain and the course of the wind.

While avalanches happen anytime, most slide in January, February, and March. That would make the most sense, since those are the true winter months. However, melting snow also causes avalanches in May and June.

Avalanches kill more than 150 people all over the world every year. A single, massive avalanche could cover 20 football fields, each piled ten feet high with snow. That would equal about 300,000 cubic yards (230,000 cu. meters) of snow!

1. What word has a silent *e* at the end?_____

2. To what does *orientation* refer? _____
_____

3. Does this article ever say exactly what an avalanche is? If not, try to make an inference._____
_____

4. What details do you have to keep in mind to figure out if an avalanche could happen?_____
_____

5. Why is this article called "The White Death"? _____
_____

Digital TV

Have you ever stuck your face up close next to your television set? If you have, you may have noticed that the picture is made of tiny dots. These dots are called pixels. Your brain is able to take those collections of small dots and reorganize them so you see one complete image.

1. What clues does the title give you about the topic of this article?_____

2. Are there any opinion words in the title? _____

3. Have you ever stuck your face right up to the TV set? If so, did you see the tiny dots?

   _____

4. Why don't you see the dots when you're at a normal distance from the TV?

   _____

A computer screen is also made of pixels, but the resolution is much higher than on your television set. Many more pixels on the screen create a picture that is crisper and much sharper. Advances in technology have led to a whole different type of signal transmission with much higher resolution—digital television.

1. What is the benefit of more pixels? _____

2. What technology takes advantage of more pixels? _____

3. What made digital TV possible? _____

4. Have you seen digital TV? If so, could you tell the difference in the picture?

   _____

Chances are the television you have in your house is an analog set. Analog means "constantly varying." Your television actually replaces the image you see every 30 seconds with a new one as it receives a variable carrier wave signal. This type of transmission is known as interlacing. Your brain is able to take those images and make continuous pictures with uninterrupted movement.

1. What is the purpose of this paragraph?_____

2. What is *interlacing*?_____

3. What does *analog* mean? _____

4. Does the author give an opinion about analog TV? _____

Digital television, however, is able to transmit much more information at a time, leading to a picture that is more stable with higher resolution. The way digital televisions can make a picture is done by progressive scan. In a progressive scan, all of the parts of the picture are transmitted at once rather than parts of the picture being replaced every 30 seconds.

1. What is the purpose of this paragraph?_____

2. What is a *progressive scan*? _____

3. What is the purpose of the author in writing this article? _____

   _____

4. How is digital television better than regular, analog television?_____

Day #1

Day #2

Day #3

Day #4

1. What clues does the title give you about the topic of this article?

   _____

Everyone's Gone to the Movies

Movies have been around longer than television and even radio. The first film technology was invented to settle a bet in 1889. Some Frenchmen said that they thought horses ran while using their front and back legs together. Other men were sure that horses ran only using the legs on either side together. The problem was that the horses ran so fast, nobody could tell for sure.

2. What was the conflict film was invented to solve? Does this paragraph tell us what the answer to the conflict was?_____

August Lumière attempted to find the solution to the horse question by taking a series of photographs of a running horse. He attached the negatives of the photographs and ran them quickly together. He shone a light behind the photographs to project them onto a screen. He created the first photographic moving image, and movies were born.

3. August Lumière created the first moving picture by
    a. using silver nitrate.
    b. shining light through photographic negatives.
    c. shooting pictures on a fast train.

Another Frenchman, Georges Méliès, saw a film produced by Lumière and was inspired to purchase a movie camera. Three months later, Méliès finished his first film. During the next 20 years, Méliès experimented with film. He used special effects that made his movie characters appear and disappear. He made many movies that had genies, ghosts, and even trips to the moon. Méliès's earliest film that still exists is titled *A Terrible Night*. It was made in 1896 and features cardboard bedbugs that keep the movie's hero awake.

Méliès directed and produced more than 500 movies, but nearly 300 were destroyed by the French military—not because they didn't like his films but because the film stock contained silver nitrate, which the military needed to prepare for World War I. In 1913, Méliès lost all his money. He operated a candy and toy booth at a train station in Paris until he retired.

4. Why did the French military destroy so many of Méliès's films? _____

   _____

5. Come up with a title that better reflects the information in the article.

   _____

Answer Key

Week #1

Name

Day #1

Diego came down with the flu on Monday night. His doctor told him to stay home from school for the rest of the week. She told him he could do schoolwork on Thursday, but not to overdo it.

1. "Over" is a prefix that means "too much" or "more than usual." So what does **over** + **do** mean? _do too much_

2. Which phrase matches the doctor's advice to Diego: ("Do schoolwork but take it easy") or "Be sure to do all your schoolwork"? Circle it.

3. How many days was Diego home not doing schoolwork? _two days_

4. Is having the flu an excuse to ignore your schoolwork? Why or why not? _It depends on how you are feeling._

Day #2

Joe and Gabby needed information for their report on (theropods.) It was hard to find resources on this (dinosaur.) They (decided) not to get (another) topic. They would leave no stone unturned while looking for information.

1. Circle all the words with three syllables.

2. What are *resources*? _sources of information_

3. Are theropods common dinosaurs to study? What detail helped you answer that question? _No. It was hard to find resources on this dinosaur._

4. Underline the correct meaning of "leave no stone unturned." a) They will turn over every stone they see to look for theropod fossils. b) They will look for information everywhere.

Day #3

Rebecca didn't finish her math (homework) last night. She played on the computer instead. She asked her mother to tell her teacher that she had been sick. Her mother told her that she would have to face the music herself.

1. Circle the compound word.

2. What is one word that says what Rebecca asked her mother to do? _lie, fib_

3. Did Rebecca make a good choice? Why or why not? _No, she should have finished her homework._

4. What does "face the music herself" mean? _Rebecca must accept the consequences of her actions._

Day #4

One morning at school, you see your friend looking dreamy-eyed. On her paper she has drawn hearts and flowers.

1. Does the beginning sound of *school* sound like the beginning sound of **skate** or **shoot**? _skate_

2. What is the opposite of *dreamy-eyed*? _down to earth, serious, practical_

3. Do you want to ask your friend about the reason for her behavior? Why or why not? _Answers will vary._

4. What do you think is happening with your friend? _She is in love._

Week #1

Name

Assessment

The Test

Billy knew that he was in trouble...big trouble. Ms. Keaton, his teacher, had seen him cheating on his test. She hadn't said anything yet, but Billy knew that she'd seen him peek at the little piece of paper hidden in his hand. He chewed on his pencil for a minute and thought. He had to get rid of that paper. But how?

"Billy, if you are finished with your test, would you please come up here?" Billy nodded. His heart was pounding so hard that he couldn't speak. He bent down to tie one of his shoes. Could he stuff the paper in his shoe? No, Ms. Keaton was watching him...waiting for him.

Billy glanced out the window. It was a beautiful spring day. But he wouldn't be going out for recess. He'd probably never get to go out for recess again. He swallowed hard. If only he had studied last night, instead of watching that TV show! Then, on the bus this morning, he decided to write down a few science facts on a piece of paper and hide it in the palm of his hand. It had been a crazy idea, and now he was going to pay for it.

Billy walked up slowly to Ms. Keaton's desk. In a flash, he had an idea! As he stood by her desk, he could open his hand so that the paper fell into her wastebasket. Later, he could try to get it back again. It was a great idea!

Ms. Keaton smiled at Billy. "Since you finished first," she said, "I thought you might like to help me set up our science experiment."

Billy was stunned. What luck! Ms. Keaton hadn't seen his little piece of paper. No all he had to do was get it into the wastebasket. As he nodded, he opened his hand. The paper fluttered down. A sudden breeze from the open window pushe[d] as it fell. It floated down to Ms. Keaton's feet.

"Billy, you dropped this," said Ms. Keaton. She picked it up. Then she looked [at] it more closely. "What exactly is this?" she asked, looking worried.

1. List two words that rhyme with *loose*. _goose, moose, truce, noose, juice_

2. Find two words in paragraph 6 that could be synonyms. _fluttered, floa[ted]_

3. Mark each of these parts of the story with an **E** for an important event or **D** for a story detail.

   _E_ a. Billy watches TV instead of studying.
   _E_ b. Ms. Keaton calls Billy up to her desk.
   _D_ c. Billy ties one of his shoes.
   _D_ d. Billy's heart pounds.
   _E_ e. Ms. Keaton picks up the paper.
   _D_ f. Billy thinks about recess.

4. Did Billy think it was a good idea to cheat on his test at the b[eg]inning of the story? Did he change his mind by the end? _Yes to both._

5. What does "pay for it" mean? _suffer the consequences_

Week #2

Name

The Underground Railroad

The Underground Railroad wasn't a railroad at all. It was a group of people who helped slaves escape to freedom. Those in charge of the escape effort were often called "conductors." The people escaping were known as "passengers." And the places where the escaping slaves stopped for help were often called "stations."

Day #1

1. What does the title tell you the subject of the selection might be? _a train that travels underground_

2. Does the opening sentence **support** or **contradict** your guess? _contradict_

3. What is the subject of this selection? _the Underground Railroad_

4. What does the opening paragraph tell us about who is involved? _conductors, passengers_

Like a train ride, the Underground Railroad moved people along. Those who escaped often followed routes that had been laid out by others before them. However, unlike a train ride, some routes went underground through dirt tunnels without any sort of tracks.

Day #2

1. What comparison does this paragraph make? _It compares the Underground Railroad with a train._

2. How is the subject like the thing it's compared with? _Both move people along._

3. How is the subject unlike the thing it's compared with? _The Underground Railroad does not move on tracks._

4. How does this paragraph make you feel? _Answers will vary._

Escaping slaves had to be certain that they could find their way. They needed food and water to make the journey. Conductors helped guide them and provide supplies. One of the most famous Underground Railroad conductors was Harriet Tubman. She had escaped slavery herself. Another famous conductor was Levi Coffin.

Day #3

1. What part of the subject does this paragraph focus on? _conductors_

2. What was their job? _to guide slaves and provide supplies_

3. Name two famous conductors. _Harriet Tubman, Levi Coffin_

4. What details did you find out about any of the conductors? _Harriet Tubman had escaped slavery herself._

Experts disagree about how well the Underground Railroad was organized. Still, it is believed that the system helped thousands of slaves reach freedom between 1830 and 1865.

Day #4

1. What problem did the Underground Railroad try to solve? _how to help slaves reach freedom_

2. What new details did you learn? _Answers will vary._

3. How many years did the Underground Railroad operate? _35 years_

4. Imagine traveling the Underground Railroad. Did you imagine yourself as the slave or the conductor? _Answers will vary._

Week #2

Name

Assessment

1. A quilt is like a sandwich: fabric as the "bread" and cotton filling as the "peanut butter." What practical reason would a person have to make a quilt?

   (a. to stay warm)   b. to use as kind[ling]   c. to eat

Quilts Reflect a Culture

Many African women knew how to sew when they came to America as slaves. They were skillful seamstresses. Sometimes these seamstresses sold for as much as $1,000 on the slavery block.

2. What was the effect of a slave's ability to sew? _She was sold for as much as $1,000, a high price._

Some slaves made quilts for their owners. They used the scraps from those quilts to make quilts for their own families. Those quilts often told the story of their families. These quilts were called story quilts.

3. Did quilts have only practical purposes for the slaves who made them? What clues from the paragraph help you answer that question? _No, quilts often told the story of their families._

A slave named Elizabeth Keckley supported 17 people by sewing. In 1855, she made enough money to buy freedom for herself and her son. That freedom cost her $1,200. She moved to Washington, D.C. There she sewed for President Lincoln's wife. She made a quilt that probably used scraps from Mrs. Lincoln's gowns.

4. How do you think Elizabeth Keckley got the scraps from Mrs. Lincoln's gowns to make her quilt? _She used the leftover scraps or pieces too small to make other clothing_

5. What do you think is the most surprising or interesting fact in the last paragraph? _Answers will vary._

Answer Key

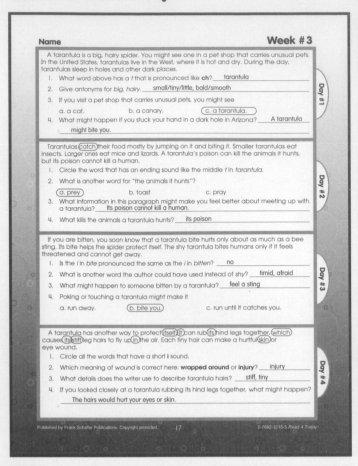

A tarantula is a big, hairy spider. You might see one in a pet shop that carries unusual pets. In the United States, tarantulas live in the West, where it is hot and dry. During the day, tarantulas sleep in holes and other dark places.

1. What word above has a *t* that is pronounced like **ch**? ___tarantula___
2. Give antonyms for *big, hairy.* ___small/tiny/little, bald/smooth___
3. If you visit a pet shop that carries unusual pets, you might see
   a. a cat.   b. a canary.   (c. a tarantula.)
4. What might happen if you stuck your hand in a dark hole in Arizona? ___A tarantula___
   ___might bite you.___

Day #1

Tarantulas (catch) their food mostly by jumping on it and biting it. Smaller tarantulas eat insects. Larger ones eat mice and lizards. A tarantula's poison can kill the animals it hunts, but its poison cannot kill a human.

1. Circle the word that has an ending sound like the middle *t* in *tarantula.*
2. What is another word for "the animals it hunts"?
   (a. prey)   b. toast   c. pray
3. What information in this paragraph might make you feel better about meeting up with a tarantula? ___Its poison cannot kill a human.___
4. What kills the animals a tarantula hunts? ___its poison___

Day #2

If you are bitten, you soon know that a tarantula bite hurts only about as much as a bee sting. Its bite helps the spider protect itself. The shy tarantula bites humans only if it feels threatened and cannot get away.

1. Is the *i* in *bite* pronounced the same as the *i* in *bitten*? ___no___
2. What is another word the author could have used instead of *shy*? ___timid, afraid___
3. What might happen to someone bitten by a tarantula? ___feel a sting___
4. Poking or touching a tarantula might make it
   a. run away.   (b. bite you.)   c. run until it catches you.

Day #3

A tarantula has another way to protect (itself.) (It) can rub (its) hind legs together, (which) causes (its) (stiff) leg hairs to fly up (in) the air. Each tiny hair can make a hurtful (skin) or eye wound.

1. Circle all the words that have a short **i** sound.
2. Which meaning of *wound* is correct here: **wrapped around** or **injury**? ___injury___
3. What details does the writer use to describe tarantula hairs? ___stiff, tiny___
4. If you looked closely at a tarantula rubbing its hind legs together, what might happen?
   ___The hairs would hurt your eyes or skin.___

Day #4

Assessment

Venus Flytrap

Kayla got a Venus flytrap for her birthday. She put it with her other plants on her windowsill. She watered all of her plants each day.

After a week, all of her plants looked fine except for the Venus flytrap. She decided that she needed more information on this plant, so she went to the library and found a book about the Venus flytrap.

She was surprised to find out that this plant was carnivorous, or meat-eating. No wonder it was not doing well! The book said that the Venus flytrap is a popular house plant. Each set of leaves stays open until an insect or piece of meat lands on the inside of the leaf. The two leaves close quickly, trapping the bait inside. After a leaf digests the meat, it dies. A new leaf grows to take the place of the dead leaf.

Now Kayla knew how to take care of her Venus flytrap.

1. Complete this sentence with a homophone of *week*: After a week the Venus flytrap was ___weak___ .
2. What does the word *carnivorous* mean? ___meat-eating___
3. What clues can you get from the compound word in the name of the *Venus flytrap* about what it might eat? ___It traps flies.___
4. Why did Kayla need to go to the library? ___She wanted to learn how to care___ ___for her Venus flytrap.___
5. What do you think Kayla will do next? ___She will feed it.___

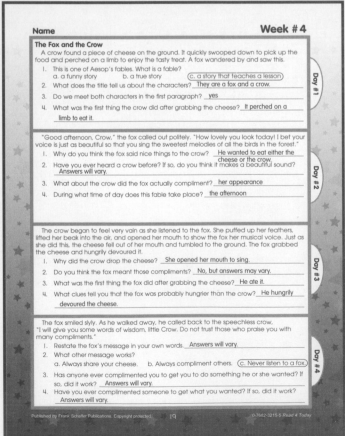

The Fox and the Crow

A crow found a piece of cheese on the ground. It quickly swooped down to pick up the food and perched on a limb to enjoy the tasty treat. A fox wandered by and saw this.

1. This is one of Aesop's fables. What is a fable?
   a. a funny story   b. a true story   (c. a story that teaches a lesson)
2. What does the title tell us about the characters? ___They are a fox and a crow.___
3. Do we meet both characters in the first paragraph? ___yes___
4. What was the first thing the crow did after grabbing the cheese? ___It perched on a___ ___limb to eat it.___

Day #1

"Good afternoon, Crow," the fox called out politely. "How lovely you look today! I bet your voice is just as beautiful so that you sing the sweetest melodies of all the birds in the forest."

1. Why do you think the fox said nice things to the crow? ___He wanted to eat either the___ ___cheese or the crow.___
2. Have you ever heard a crow before? If so, do you think it makes a beautiful sound? ___Answers will vary.___
3. What about the crow did the fox actually compliment? ___her appearance___
4. During what time of day does this fable take place? ___the afternoon___

Day #2

The crow began to feel very vain as she listened to the fox. She puffed up her feathers, lifted her beak into the air, and opened her mouth to show the fox her musical voice. Just as she did this, the cheese fell out of her mouth and tumbled to the ground. The fox grabbed the cheese and hungrily devoured it.

1. Why did the crow drop the cheese? ___She opened her mouth to sing.___
2. Do you think the fox meant those compliments? ___No, but answers may vary.___
3. What was the first thing the fox did after grabbing the cheese? ___He ate it.___
4. What clues tell you that the fox was probably hungrier than the crow? ___He hungrily___ ___devoured the cheese.___

Day #3

The fox smiled slyly. As he walked away, he called back to the speechless crow, "I will give you some words of wisdom, little Crow. Do not trust those who praise you with many compliments."

1. Restate the fox's message in your own words. ___Answers will vary.___
2. What other message works?
   a. Always share your cheese.   b. Always compliment others.   (c. Never listen to a fox.)
3. Has anyone ever complimented you to get you to do something he or she wanted? If so, did it work? ___Answers will vary.___
4. Have you ever complimented someone to get what you wanted? If so, did it work? ___Answers will vary.___

Day #4

Assessment

1. By reading the title, do you think this is one of Aesop's fables? ___yes___

The Oak and the Reeds

A mighty oak grew along a riverbank. Its trunk was thick, and its branches reached upward into the sky. It towered proudly above a patch of reeds that grew below it along the edge of the water.

2. What type of objects are the two characters in this fable? ___plants___

On most days, a breeze blew across the river. The leaves of the mighty oak danced, but its branches held firmly in place. The oak laughed at the reeds because the wind was not so kind to them. The reeds trembled and shook as they struggled to stand up straight. But the reeds did not mind the laughter of the oak; after all, the tree was so much bigger and stronger.

Then one day, a terrible hurricane approached the river. Its violent winds pulled up the roots of the mighty oak and tossed it to the ground. When the storm was over, the great tree lay in the patch of reeds.

3. How is the oak tree different from the reeds? ___The oak tree is bigger and stronger and does not bend. The reeds___ ___are smaller and bend easily.___

The oak spoke sadly, "The strong winds were able to pick me up and throw me to the ground like a stick. Yet you reeds were able to stay rooted even though you are much smaller. How could this be?"

One reed spoke. "We may be small, but we know how to bend, whether the wind blows gently or violently. You, mighty oak, were too proud and did not know how to bend."

4. What caused the oak tree to fall? ___violent winds of the hurricane___
5. What is the lesson of this fable?
   (a. It can be better to be flexible than to be strong.)
   b. It's okay to laugh at those smaller than you.
   c. Stay out of the way of a hurricane.

Answer Key

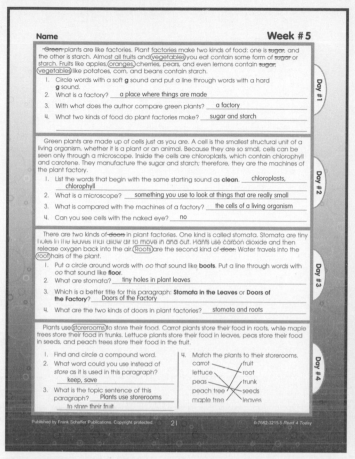

~~Green~~ plants are like factories. Plant factories make two kinds of food: one is sugar, and the other is starch. Almost all fruits and (vegetables) you eat contain some form of ~~sugar~~ or starch. Fruits like apples, (oranges,) cherries, pears, and even lemons contain ~~sugar~~. (vegetables) like potatoes, corn, and beans contain starch.

Day #1

1. Circle words with a soft **g** sound and put a line through words with a hard **g** sound.
2. What is a factory? <u>a place where things are made</u>
3. With what does the author compare green plants? <u>a factory</u>
4. What two kinds of food do plant factories make? <u>sugar and starch</u>

Green plants are made up of cells just as you are. A cell is the smallest structural unit of a living organism, whether it is a plant or an animal. Because they are so small, cells can be seen only through a microscope. Inside the cells are chloroplasts, which contain chlorophyll and carotene. They manufacture the sugar and starch; therefore, they are the machines of the plant factory.

Day #2

1. List the words that begin with the same starting sound as **clean**. <u>chloroplasts,</u> <u>chlorophyll</u>
2. What is a microscope? <u>something you use to look at things that are really small</u>
3. What is compared with the machines of a factory? <u>the cells of a living organism</u>
4. Can you see cells with the naked eye? <u>no</u>

There are two kinds of ~~doors~~ in plant factories. One kind is called stomata. Stomata are tiny holes in the leaves that allow air to move in and out. Plants use carbon dioxide and then release oxygen back into the air. (Roots) are the second kind of ~~door~~. Water travels into the (root) hairs of the plant.

Day #3

1. Put a circle around words with **oo** that sound like **boots**. Put a line through words with **oo** that sound like **floor**.
2. What are stomata? <u>tiny holes in plant leaves</u>
3. Which is a better title for this paragraph: **Stomata in the Leaves** or **Doors of the Factory**? <u>Doors of the Factory</u>
4. What are the two kinds of doors in plant factories? <u>stomata and roots</u>

Plants use (storerooms) to store their food. Carrot plants store their food in roots, while maple trees store their food in trunks. Lettuce plants store their food in leaves, peas store their food in seeds, and peach trees store their food in the fruit.

Day #4

1. Find and circle a compound word.
2. What word could you use instead of *store* as it is used in this paragraph? <u>keep, save</u>
3. What is the topic sentence of this paragraph? <u>Plants use storerooms to store their food</u>
4. Match the plants to their storerooms.

carrot — fruit
lettuce — root
peas — trunk
peach tree — seeds
maple tree — leaves

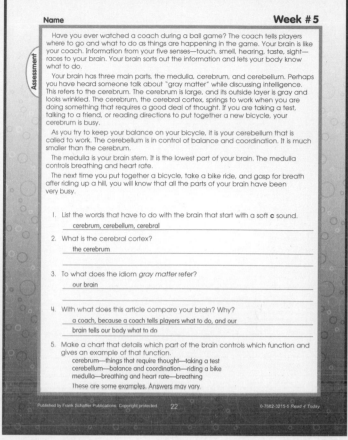

Assessment

Have you ever watched a coach during a ball game? The coach tells players where to go and what to do as things are happening in the game. Your brain is like your coach. Information from your five senses—touch, smell, hearing, taste, sight—races to your brain. Your brain sorts out the information and lets your body know what to do.

Your brain has three main parts, the medulla, cerebrum, and cerebellum. Perhaps you have heard someone talk about "gray matter" while discussing intelligence. This refers to the cerebrum. The cerebrum is large, and its outside layer is gray and looks wrinkled. The cerebrum, the cerebral cortex, springs to work when you are doing something that requires a good deal of thought. If you are taking a test, talking to a friend, or reading directions to put together a new bicycle, your cerebrum is busy.

As you try to keep your balance on your bicycle, it is your cerebellum that is called to work. The cerebellum is in control of balance and coordination. It is much smaller than the cerebrum.

The medulla is your brain stem. It is the lowest part of your brain. The medulla controls breathing and heart rate.

The next time you put together a bicycle, take a bike ride, and gasp for breath after riding up a hill, you will know that all the parts of your brain have been very busy.

1. List the words that have to do with the brain that start with a soft **c** sound. <u>cerebrum, cerebellum, cerebral</u>
2. What is the cerebral cortex? <u>the cerebrum</u>
3. To what does the idiom *gray matter* refer? <u>our brain</u>
4. With what does this article compare your brain? Why? <u>a coach, because a coach tells players what to do, and our brain tells our body what to do</u>
5. Make a chart that details which part of the brain controls which function and gives an example of that function.
<u>cerebrum—things that require thought—taking a test</u>
<u>cerebellum—balance and coordination—riding a bike</u>
<u>medulla—breathing and heart rate—breathing</u>
<u>These are some examples. Answers may vary.</u>

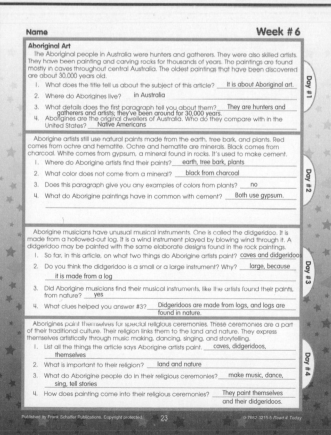

Aboriginal Art

The Aboriginal people in Australia were hunters and gatherers. They were also skilled artists. They have been painting and carving rocks for thousands of years. The paintings are found mostly in caves throughout central Australia. The oldest paintings that have been discovered are about 30,000 years old.

Day #1

1. What does the title tell us about the subject of this article? <u>It is about Aboriginal art.</u>
2. Where do Aborigines live? <u>in Australia</u>
3. What details does the first paragraph tell you about them? <u>They are hunters and gatherers and artists; they've been around for 30,000 years.</u>
4. Aborigines are the original dwellers of Australia. Who do they compare with in the United States? <u>Native Americans</u>

Aborigine artists still use natural paints made from the earth, tree bark, and plants. Red comes from ochre and hematite. Ochre and hematite are minerals. Black comes from charcoal. White comes from gypsum, a mineral found in rocks. It's used to make cement.

Day #2

1. Where do Aborigine artists find their paints? <u>earth, tree bark, plants</u>
2. What color does not come from a mineral? <u>black from charcoal</u>
3. Does this paragraph give you any examples of colors from plants? <u>no</u>
4. What do Aborigine paintings have in common with cement? <u>Both use gypsum.</u>

Aborigine musicians have unusual musical instruments. One is called the didgeridoo. It is made from a hollowed-out log. It is a wind instrument played by blowing wind through it. A didgeridoo may be painted with the same elaborate designs found in the rock paintings.

Day #3

1. So far, in this article, on what two things do Aborigine artists paint? <u>caves and didgeridoos</u>
2. Do you think the didgeridoo is a small or a large instrument? Why? <u>large, because it is made from a log</u>
3. Did Aborigine musicians find their musical instruments, like the artists found their paints, from nature? <u>yes</u>
4. What clues helped you answer #3? <u>Didgeridoos are made from logs, and logs are found in nature.</u>

Aborigines paint themselves for special religious ceremonies. These ceremonies are a part of their traditional culture. Their religion links them to the land and nature. They express themselves artistically through music making, dancing, singing, and storytelling.

Day #4

1. List all the things the article says Aborigine artists paint. <u>caves, didgeridoos, themselves</u>
2. What is important to their religion? <u>land and nature</u>
3. What do Aborigine people do in their religious ceremonies? <u>make music, dance, sing, tell stories</u>
4. How does painting come into their religious ceremonies? <u>They paint themselves and their didgeridoos.</u>

---

1. What would you guess the topic of this article is, based on the title? <u>Answers may vary but should be something about dreaming or sleeping.</u>

Assessment

Dreamtime

The Aborigines have been in Australia for thousands of years. Some scientists believe they have been there about 30,000 years. The name *Aborigine* means "the very first." They were the very first people in Australia. The Aborigines believe that ancestral beings created the world in a time very long ago, called Dreamtime. Elders know the history of Dreamtime. They pass it on to younger generations.

2. What is the Dreamtime in this article? Was it what you expected from the title? <u>Dreamtime is the time when Aborigines believe the world was created.</u> <u>No, it was different from what I expected.</u>

Dreamtime explains the beginning of the world. Aborigines believe that during Dreamtime, spirits created the land, animals, plants, and humans. The spirit beings didn't die. They joined with nature. They live in the Aborigine beliefs and sacred rituals. Dreamtime explains the rules for living. It explains the rules for social behavior. It explains the whole structure of society.

3. List all the things the second paragraph says Aborigines believe Dreamtime explains. <u>the beginning of the world, rules for living, rules for social behavior, structure of society</u>

Dreamtime paintings are usually symmetrical. They are made of arcs, circles, and ovals. Some lines are straight. Some are curved. Specific patterns and designs have names. The men paint Dreamtime symbols and patterns on their bodies for special ceremonies. The ceremonies are called corroborees.

4. Name the geometrical shapes used in Dreamtime paintings. <u>arc, circle, oval</u>

5. What clues from the article tell you that Dreamtime has a central place in Aborigine life and culture? <u>it explains the beginning of the world and everything about Aboriginal life, and the spirits that created the world still live in nature and in their rituals</u>

Answer Key

Day #1

Teddy just about fell out of his seat. Mrs. Beeker, his science teacher, announced that during the following week the class would go to the Colgate Nature Preserve to examine pond life! That meant he'd be free to splash away in the water in search of his beloved leopard frogs!

1. Which letter in *leopard* is silent?   the "o"
2. When is *the following week*?
   a. that week   (b. the next week)   c. two weeks from then
3. What effect did the setting of his class trip have on Teddy?   He was excited.
4. What do you think a leopard frog looks like?   A frog with spots like a leopard.

Day #2

The next week, the class boarded a waiting bus and rode off to the rural setting of Dilly Pond. Students scooped and trowled for larvae, crustaceans, and small fish. They observed birds, mammals, and amphibians in the wetlands. And Teddy mucked around in the rushes among the creatures of frog heaven.

1. Which word ends with the same ending as *oceans*?   crustaceans
2. Does *rural* mean **in the city** or **in the country**?   in the country
3. List all the items the kids interacted with in the wetlands.   larvae, crustaceans, small fish, plants, birds, mammals, amphibians, frogs
4. What does the author mean by *frog heaven*?   Suggested answers: A place where frogs thrive; an ideal place where the main character can study frogs.

Day #3

That was thirty years ago. But Teddy still remembers. As he prepares the science laboratory for his students, his mind returns to the pond that glorious fall day so many years ago. It was the day that he first knew what he wanted to do with his life. It was one of the best days he could remember.

1. Does the *ou* in *glorious* sound like the *ou* in **out** or **serious**?   serious
2. What other word (two syllables or more) could you use instead of *glorious*?   fabulous, fantastic, gorgeous, beautiful
3. What is Teddy's job today?   science teacher
4. What effect did the field trip to Dilly's Pond have on Teddy's life?   It made him want to be a science teacher.

Day #4

With a whimper, Daisy hung her head and looked at me beseechingly.

1. *Beseechingly* has two suffixes. What are they?   –ing and –ly
2. When Daisy looks beseechingly, is she **begging** or **angry**?   begging
3. Does Daisy sound happy? What clues helped you answer that question?   no; she whimpered / cried and hung her head
4. What do you think Daisy is?   a dog

Assessment

Aquarium Competition

Jake opened the lid of his aquarium. Most of the fish quickly swam to the top. They knew it was time for dinner. Jake paused before sprinkling the food across the water. He noticed that one little fish stayed away from the others. Its fins were looking ragged. Jake wondered whether the fish might be sick.

Jake tapped the can, and the food fell out. He saw one big fish rush to the top and gobble up most of the food. This same fish nipped at the fins of the smaller fish whenever it tried to grab a bite.

"I see why its fins are ragged," thought Jake. "That little fish isn't sick at all. The bigger fish is just picking on it."

Jake got out a smaller fish bowl. He poured some tank water into the bowl, scooped the ragged fish out of the aquarium with a net, and gently put it in the small bowl.

"There you go, little guy!" said Jake. "I'll give you lots of food and some time to grow. When you get big and strong, I'll put you back in the aquarium again. Then you will be able to compete with that bully fish!"

1. Find a word that begins with a soft **g** sound.   gently
2. What does it mean to be a bully?   A bully uses force to make others (people or fish) do what it wants.
3. What is the effect of the big fish gobbling up all the food?   The little fish didn't get enough food and was scared of the big fish.
4. In this story, what does *compete* mean?
   (a. to get to the top of the tank faster)
   b. to be a bigger bully
   c. to grow bigger than the others
5. Try to predict what will happen to the little, ragged fish now.   It will grow bigger because it won't have to compete for its food.

Those Wacky Australian Animals

Australia's animals are unique. They include marsupials and monotremes. Both are mammals. Marsupials carry their babies in pouches. Monotremes give birth to their young by laying eggs, but they produce milk to feed their babies.

Day #1

1. What clues does the title give us about the subject of this article?   It will be about Australian animals that the author thinks are wacky.
2. What word in the title tells us the author has a sense of humor about the article?   wacky
3. What is distinctive about monotremes?   mammals that lay eggs
4. What is distinctive about marsupials?   babies are carried in mom's pouch

The Tasmanian devil is a ferocious marsupial that lives on the island of Tasmania. These animals have black fur and very sharp teeth. They eat other mammals, birds, and reptiles.

Day #2

1. What kind of animal is the Tasmanian devil?   marsupial, carnivore
2. What clues does the paragraph give you that it deserves the name *devil*?   It has sharp teeth and eats other mammals, birds, and reptiles.
3. How did the *Tasmanian* part of its name come about?   It lives on the island of Tasmania.
4. Is the Tasmanian devil a carnivore?   yes

The duck-billed platypus is one of two animals that hatches its young from eggs. It has soft fur, a snout, webbed feet and claws, and a flat tail like a beaver's tail. They live near rivers and creeks, where they eat crawfish, worms, and small fish.

Day #3

1. What kind of animal is the duck-billed platypus?   monotreme, carnivore
2. What animal is compared with the duck-billed platypus in the paragraph?   beaver
3. Look at the list of characteristics of the duck-billed platypus. List other animals that share one characteristic. You may want to make a chart.   One example: soft fur—kitten
4. What do you think of the duck-billed platypus's looks?   Answers will vary.

Kangaroos are herbivores. Baby kangaroos, called joeys, live in their mother's pouch for 5 to 6 months. Kangaroos can hop at about 40 miles per hour (about 64.3 kph). They have strong hind legs for leaping about 30 to 40 feet (about 9 to 12 m).

Day #4

1. What does an herbivore eat?
   a. meat   (b. plants)   c. metal
2. What kind of animal is a kangaroo?   herbivore, marsupial
3. How does a kangaroo get around?   It hops on its hind legs.
4. Is the author right? Are some Australian animals wacky?   yes; answers may vary.

Assessment

1. This title gives a lot of information. What does it tell us the author will do in this article?   The author will compare Australia and the United States.

Australia and the United States: Alike or Different?

How are Australia and the United States alike? How are they different? Australia is in the Southern Hemisphere. The United States is in the Northern Hemisphere. Australia's summer months are December through February, which are the United States' winter months. Summer months in the U.S. are June through August, which are Australia's winter months. In the Northern Hemisphere, hurricanes and tornadoes spin in a clockwise direction. In the Southern Hemisphere, they spin in a counterclockwise direction.

2. Suppose that your birthday is December 11. Compare the activities you could do at your birthday party if you lived in Australia and if you lived in the United States.   Answers will vary, but one example would be a beach party in Australia and a skating party in the United States.

Australians drive on the left side of the road, while people in the United States drive on the right side of the road. Australia's population is about 19 million. That's about the same as the total of the six most populated cities in the United States. Australia has kangaroos, anteaters, emus, and koalas, but in the United States you'll find those animals only in zoos.

3. Do more people live in Australia or in the United States?   United States

The official head of Australia's government is the queen of England. In the United States, it is the president. Australians elect people to a legislature, and a prime minister is the functional head of government. There are three major political parties there, but only two in the U.S. An Australian law says that people who are able to vote must vote. If not, they can be fined. There's no law like that in the United States.

4. Put the following topics in the order they appear in the article: population, politics, climate, wildlife, customs.   climate, customs, population, wildlife, politics
5. What do you think is the most interesting difference between Australia and the United States?   Answers will vary.

Answer Key

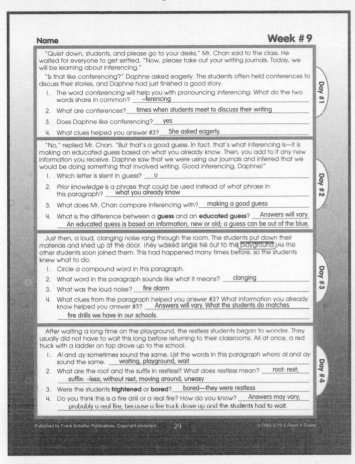

"Quiet down, students, and please go to your desks," Mr. Chan said to the class. He waited for everyone to get settled. "Now, please take out your writing journals. Today, we will be learning about inferencing."

"Is that like conferencing?" Daphne asked eagerly. The students often held conferences to discuss their stories, and Daphne had just finished a good story.

Day #1

1. The word *conferencing* will help you with pronouncing *inferencing*. What do the two words share in common? __–ferencing__
2. What are conferences? __times when students meet to discuss their writing__
3. Does Daphne like conferencing? __yes__
4. What clues helped you answer #3? __She asked eagerly.__

"No," replied Mr. Chan. "But that's a good guess. In fact, that's what inferencing is—it is making an educated guess based on what you already know. Then, you add to it any new information you receive. Daphne saw that we were using our journals and inferred that we would be doing something that involved writing. Good inferencing, Daphne!"

Day #2

1. Which letter is silent in *guess*? __u__
2. *Prior knowledge* is a phrase that could be used instead of what phrase in this paragraph? __what you already know__
3. What does Mr. Chan compare inferencing with? __making a good guess__
4. What is the difference between a **guess** and an **educated guess**? __Answers will vary.__ __An educated guess is based on information, new or old; a guess can be out of the blue.__

Just then, a loud, clanging noise rang through the room. The students put down their materials and lined up at the door. They walked single file out to the playground. All the other students soon joined them. This had happened many times before, so the students knew what to do.

Day #3

1. Circle a compound word in this paragraph.
2. What word in this paragraph sounds like what it means? __clanging__
3. What was the loud noise? __fire alarm__
4. What clues from the paragraph helped you answer #3? What information you already know helped you answer #3? __Answers will vary. What the students do matches__ __fire drills we have in our schools.__

After waiting a long time on the playground, the restless students began to wonder. They usually did not have to wait this long before returning to their classrooms. All at once, a red truck with a ladder on top drove up to the school.

Day #4

1. *Ai* and *ay* sometimes sound the same. List the words in this paragraph where *ai* and *ay* sound the same. __waiting, playground, wait__
2. What are the root and the suffix in *restless*? What does *restless* mean? __root: rest;__ __suffix: -less; without rest, moving around, uneasy__
3. Were the students **frightened** or **bored**? __bored—they were restless__
4. Do you think this is a fire drill or a real fire? How do you know? __Answers may vary;__ __probably a real fire, because a fire truck drove up and the students had to wait.__

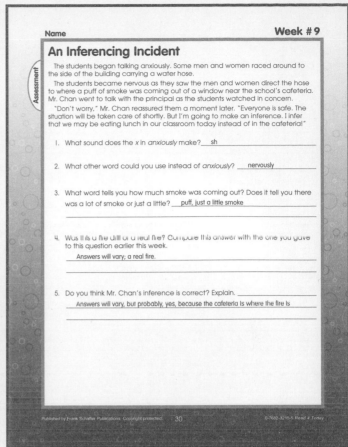

An Inferencing Incident

Assessment

The students began talking anxiously. Some men and women raced around to the side of the building carrying a water hose.

The students became nervous as they saw the men and women direct the hose to where a puff of smoke was coming out of a window near the school's cafeteria. Mr. Chan went to talk with the principal as the students watched in concern.

"Don't worry," Mr. Chan reassured them a moment later. "Everyone is safe. The situation will be taken care of shortly. But I'm going to make an inference. I infer that we may be eating lunch in our classroom today instead of in the cafeteria!"

1. What sound does the *x* in *anxiously* make? __sh__

2. What other word could you use instead of *anxiously*? __nervously__

3. What word tells you how much smoke was coming out? Does it tell you there was a lot of smoke or just a little? __puff, just a little smoke__

4. Was this a fire drill or a real fire? Compare this answer with the one you gave to this question earlier this week. __Answers will vary; a real fire.__

5. Do you think Mr. Chan's inference is correct? Explain. __Answers will vary, but probably, yes, because the cafeteria is where the fire is__

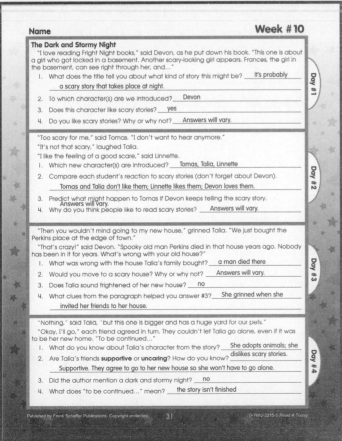

The Dark and Stormy Night

"I love reading Fright Night books," said Devon, as he put down his book. "This one is about a girl who got locked in a basement. Another scary-looking girl appears. Frances, the girl in the basement, can see right through her, and..."

Day #1

1. What does the title tell you about what kind of story this might be? __It's probably__ __a scary story that takes place at night.__
2. To which character(s) are we introduced? __Devon__
3. Does this character like scary stories? __yes__
4. Do you like scary stories? Why or why not? __Answers will vary.__

"Too scary for me," said Tomas. "I don't want to hear anymore."

"It's not that scary," laughed Talia. said Linnette.

"I like the feeling of a good scare," said Linnette.

Day #2

1. Which new character(s) are introduced? __Tomas, Talia, Linnette__
2. Compare each student's reaction to scary stories (don't forget about Devon). __Tomas and Talia don't like them; Linnette likes them; Devon loves them.__
3. Predict what might happen to Tomas if Devon keeps telling the scary story. __Answers will vary.__
4. Why do you think people like to read scary stories? __Answers will vary.__

"Then you wouldn't mind going to my new house," grinned Talia. "We just bought the Perkins place at the edge of town."

"That's crazy!" said Devon. "Spooky old man Perkins died in that house years ago. Nobody has been in it for years. What's wrong with your old house?"

Day #3

1. What was wrong with the house Talia's family bought? __a man died there__
2. Would you move to a scary house? Why or why not? __Answers will vary.__
3. Does Talia sound frightened of her new house? __no__
4. What clues from the paragraph helped you answer #3? __She grinned when she__ __invited her friends to her house.__

"Nothing," said Talia, "but this one is bigger and has a huge yard for our pets."

"Okay, I'll go," each friend agreed in turn. They couldn't let Talia go alone, even if it was to be her new home. "To be continued..."

Day #4

1. What do you know about Talia's character from the story? __She adopts animals; she dislikes scary stories.__
2. Are Talia's friends **supportive** or **uncaring**? How do you know? __Supportive. They agree to go to her new house so she won't have to go alone.__
3. Did the author mention a dark and stormy night? __no__
4. What does "to be continued..." mean? __the story isn't finished__

1. What does the title tell you about what this story will be about? __It will be the continuation of a scary story.__

The Dark and Stormy Night: Part Two

Assessment

The friends met and rode their bikes to the old Perkins house after dinner. It didn't look so bad in the twilight. Suddenly, it began to rain, then thunder and lightning crashed through the sky, which quickly turned dark.

"Oh, no!" said Devon. "It's a dark and stormy night. Something awful is going to happen. And I just thought of something else. It's Friday the thirteenth!"

2. Is there any new information in the above paragraphs that make sense of the title? If so, what? __Yes, the night turned dark and stormy.__

The group turned their bikes around and began to leave. Just then a tree fell to the ground and blocked their exit. "We'll have to go in the house," said Talia. They got off their bikes and followed her as if going to their doom. When Talia opened the door, it creaked. Suddenly they heard footsteps walking towards them. The friends looked for a place to hide, but it was too dark. "Ouch!" said Linnette as she bumped into a wall. Everyone began to scream.

"What's going on?" said a voice.

3. What details make this paragraph scary? __a tree falls so they can't leave,__ __the door creaks, it's dark and they hear footsteps, they scream__

The lights went on. The house was warm and cozy and filled with furniture. The storm seemed far away. The old Perkins place had changed from the neighborhood haunted house into the perfect place for Talia's family.

"Welcome to our new home," said Talia's dad. "Talia told us she was bringing you all. I think maybe she didn't tell you we were settled here already. Have some hot chocolate and cookies. It's a dark and stormy night out there. Call your parents and ask them if you can stay a while. After all, tomorrow is Saturday."

The group looked around the room. Talia was lucky. "Come on, I'll give you a tour," Talia said proudly. "This place is full of nooks and crannies and secret places, thanks to Mr. Perkins. We can pick one and sit to tell ghost stories."

"I think I've had enough scary stuff for tonight," said Linnette.

"This is more fun than a Fright Night book," said Devon. And everyone agreed.

4. What negative did Talia's dad turn into a positive? __The negative was that the house was scary because of Mr. Perkins, Talia's dad says it's fun because of Mr. Perkins.__
5. Write a different ending for the story. __Answers will vary.__

Answer Key

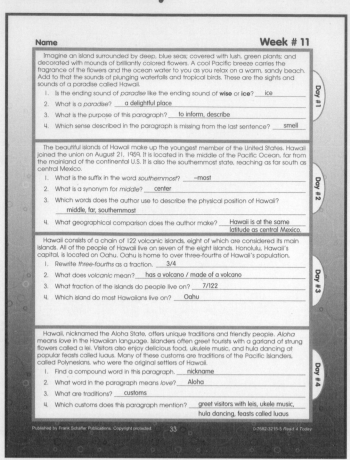

Imagine an island surrounded by deep, blue seas; covered with lush, green plants; and decorated with mounds of brilliantly colored flowers. A cool Pacific breeze carries the fragrance of the flowers and the ocean water to you as you relax on a warm, sandy beach. Add to that the sounds of plunging waterfalls and tropical birds. These are the sights and sounds of a paradise called Hawaii.

Day #1

1. Is the ending sound of *paradise* like the ending sound of **wise** or **ice**? ice
2. What is a *paradise*? a delightful place
3. What is the purpose of this paragraph? to inform, describe
4. Which sense described in the paragraph is missing from the last sentence? smell

The beautiful islands of Hawaii make up the youngest member of the United States. Hawaii joined the union on August 21, 1959. It is located in the middle of the Pacific Ocean, far from the mainland of the continental U.S. It is also the southernmost state, reaching as far south as central Mexico.

Day #2

1. What is the suffix in the word *southernmost*? –most
2. What is a synonym for *middle*? center
3. Which words does the author use to describe the physical position of Hawaii? middle, far, southernmost
4. What geographical comparison does the author make? Hawaii is at the same latitude as central Mexico.

Hawaii consists of a chain of 122 volcanic islands, eight of which are considered its main islands. All of the people of Hawaii live on seven of the eight islands. Honolulu, Hawaii's capital, is located on Oahu. Oahu is home to over three-fourths of Hawaii's population.

Day #3

1. Rewrite *three-fourths* as a fraction. 3/4
2. What does *volcanic* mean? has a volcano / made of a volcano
3. What fraction of the islands do people live on? 7/122
4. Which island do most Hawaiians live on? Oahu

Hawaii, nicknamed the Aloha State, offers unique traditions and friendly people. *Aloha* means *love* in the Hawaiian language. Islanders often greet tourists with a garland of strung flowers called a lei. Visitors also enjoy delicious food, ukulele music, and hula dancing at popular feasts called luaus. Many of these customs are traditions of the Pacific Islanders, called Polynesians, who were the original settlers of Hawaii.

Day #4

1. Find a compound word in this paragraph. nickname
2. What word in the paragraph means *love*? Aloha
3. What are traditions? customs
4. Which customs does this paragraph mention? greet visitors with leis, ukele music, hula dancing, feasts called luaus

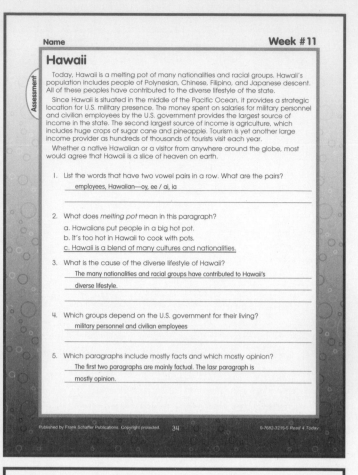

Hawaii

Assessment

Today, Hawaii is a melting pot of many nationalities and racial groups. Hawaii's population includes people of Polynesian, Chinese, Filipino, and Japanese descent. All of these peoples have contributed to the diverse lifestyle of the state.

Since Hawaii is situated in the middle of the Pacific Ocean, it provides a strategic location for U.S. military presence. The money spent on salaries for military personnel and civilian employees by the U.S. government provides the largest source of income in the state. The second largest source of income is agriculture, which includes huge crops of sugar cane and pineapple. Tourism is yet another large income provider as hundreds of thousands of tourists visit each year.

Whether a native Hawaiian or a visitor from anywhere around the globe, most would agree that Hawaii is a slice of heaven on earth.

1. List the words that have two vowel pairs in a row. What are the pairs?
   employees, Hawaiian—oy, ee / ai, ia

2. What does *melting pot* mean in this paragraph?
   a. Hawaiians put people in a big hot pot.
   b. It's too hot in Hawaii to cook with pots.
   c. Hawaii is a blend of many cultures and nationalities.

3. What is the cause of the diverse lifestyle of Hawaii?
   The many nationalities and racial groups have contributed to Hawaii's diverse lifestyle.

4. Which groups depend on the U.S. government for their living?
   military personnel and civilian employees

5. Which paragraphs include mostly facts and which mostly opinion?
   The first two paragraphs are mainly factual. The lasr paragraph is mostly opinion.

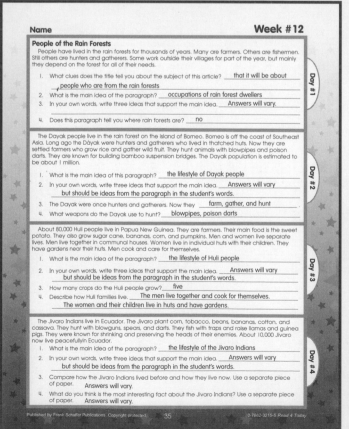

People of the Rain Forests

People have lived in the rain forests for thousands of years. Many are farmers. Others are fishermen. Still others are hunters and gatherers. Some work outside their villages for part of the year, but mainly they depend on the forest for all of their needs.

Day #1

1. What clues does the title tell you about the subject of this article? that it will be about people who are from the rain forests
2. What is the main idea of the paragraph? occupations of rain forest dwellers
3. In your own words, write three ideas that support the main idea. Answers will vary.
4. Does this paragraph tell you where rain forests are? no

The Dayak people live in the rain forest on the island of Borneo. Borneo is off the coast of Southeast Asia. Long ago the Dayak were hunters and gatherers who lived in thatched huts. Now they are settled farmers who grow rice and gather wild fruit. They hunt animals with blowpipes and poison darts. They are known for building bamboo suspension bridges. The Dayak population is estimated to be about 1 million.

Day #2

1. What is the main idea of this paragraph? the lifestyle of Dayak people
2. In your own words, write three ideas that support the main idea. Answers will vary but should be ideas from the paragraph in the student's words.
3. The Dayak were once hunters and gatherers. Now they farm, gather, and hunt.
4. What weapons do the Dayak use to hunt? blowpipes, poison darts

About 80,000 Huli people live in Papua New Guinea. They are farmers. Their main food is the sweet potato. They also grow sugar cane, bananas, corn, and pumpkins. Men and women live separate lives. Men live together in communal houses. Women live in individual huts with their children. They have gardens near their huts. Men cook and care for themselves.

Day #3

1. What is the main idea of the paragraph? the lifestyle of Huli people
2. In your own words, write three ideas that support the main idea. Answers will vary but should be ideas from the paragraph in the student's words.
3. How many crops do the Huli people grow? five
4. Describe how Huli families live. The men live together and cook for themselves. The women and their children live in huts and have gardens.

The Jivaro Indians live in Ecuador. The Jivaro plant corn, tobacco, beans, bananas, cotton, and cassava. They hunt with blowguns, spears, and darts. They fish with traps and raise llamas and guinea pigs. They were known for shrinking and preserving the heads of their enemies. About 10,000 Jivaro now live peacefully in Ecuador.

Day #4

1. What is the main idea of the paragraph? the lifestyle of the Jivaro Indians
2. In your own words, write three ideas that support the main idea. Answers will vary but should be ideas from the paragraph in the student's words.
3. Compare how the Jivaro Indians lived before and how they live now. Use a separate piece of paper. Answers will vary.
4. What do you think is the most interesting fact about the Jivaro Indians? Use a separate piece of paper. Answers will vary.

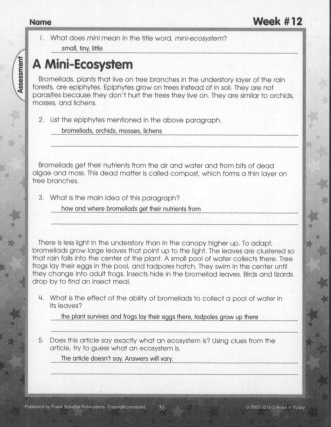

Assessment

1. What does *mini* mean in the title word, *mini-ecosystem*? small, tiny, little

A Mini-Ecosystem

Bromeliads, plants that live on tree branches in the understory layer of the rain forests, are epiphytes. Epiphytes grow on trees instead of in soil. They are not parasites because they don't hurt the trees they live on. They are similar to orchids, mosses, and lichens.

2. List the epiphytes mentioned in the above paragraph.
   bromeliads, orchids, mosses, lichens

Bromeliads get their nutrients from the air and water and from bits of dead algae and moss. This dead matter is called compost, which forms a thin layer on tree branches.

3. What is the main idea of this paragraph?
   how and where bromeliads get their nutrients from

There is less light in the understory than in the canopy higher up. To adapt, bromeliads grow large leaves that point up to the light. The leaves are clustered so that rain falls into the center of the plant. A small pool of water collects there. Tree frogs lay their eggs in the pool, and tadpoles hatch. They swim in the center until they change into adult frogs. Insects hide in the bromeliad leaves. Birds and lizards drop by for an insect meal.

4. What is the effect of the ability of bromeliads to collect a pool of water in its leaves?
   the plant survives and frogs lay their eggs there, tadpoles grow up there

5. Does this article say exactly what an ecosystem is? Using clues from the article, try to guess what an ecosystem is.
   The article doesn't say. Answers will vary.

Answer Key

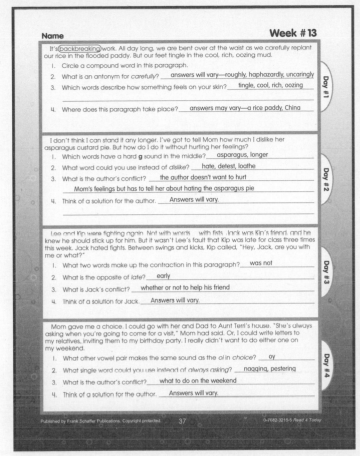

It's (backbreaking) work. All day long, we are bent over at the waist as we carefully replant our rice in the flooded paddy. But our feet tingle in the cool, rich, oozing mud.

Day #1

1. Circle a compound word in this paragraph.
2. What is an antonym for *carefully*? __answers will vary—roughly, haphazardly, uncaringly__
3. Which words describe how something feels on your skin? __tingle, cool, rich, oozing__
4. Where does this paragraph take place? __answers may vary—a rice paddy, China__

I don't think I can stand it any longer. I've got to tell Mom how much I dislike her asparagus custard pie. But how do I do it without hurting her feelings?

Day #2

1. Which words have a hard **g** sound in the middle? __asparagus, longer__
2. What word could you use instead of *dislike*? __hate, detest, loathe__
3. What is the author's conflict? __the author doesn't want to hurt Mom's feelings but has to tell her about hating the asparagus pie__
4. Think of a solution for the author. __Answers will vary.__

Lee and Kip were fighting again. Not with words — with fists. Jack was Kip's friend, and he knew he should stick up for him. But it wasn't Lee's fault that Kip was late for class three times this week. Jack hated fights. Between swings and kicks, Kip called, "Hey, Jack, are you with me or what?"

Day #3

1. What two words make up the contraction in this paragraph? __was not__
2. What is the opposite of *late*? __early__
3. What is Jack's conflict? __whether or not to help his friend__
4. Think of a solution for Jack. __Answers will vary.__

Mom gave me a choice. I could go with her and Dad to Aunt Terri's house. "She's always asking when you're going to come for a visit," Mom had said. Or, I could write letters to my relatives, inviting them to my birthday party. I really didn't want to do either one on my weekend.

Day #4

1. What other vowel pair makes the same sound as the *oi* in *choice*? __oy__
2. What single word could you use instead of *always asking*? __nagging, pestering__
3. What is the author's conflict? __what to do on the weekend__
4. Think of a solution for the author. __Answers will vary.__

Assessment

Score!

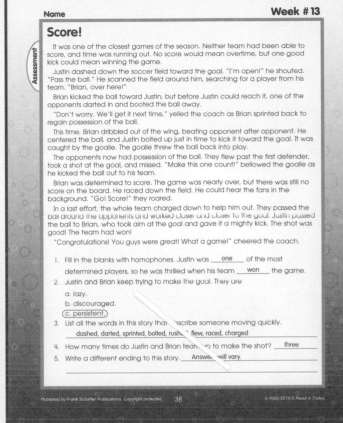

It was one of the closest games of the season. Neither team had been able to score, and time was running out. No score would mean overtime, but one good kick could mean winning the game.

Justin dashed down the soccer field toward the goal. "I'm open!" he shouted. "Pass the ball." He scanned the field around him, searching for a player from his team. "Brian, over here!"

Brian kicked the ball toward Justin, but before Justin could reach it, one of the opponents darted in and booted the ball away.

"Don't worry. We'll get it next time," yelled the coach as Brian sprinted back to regain possession of the ball.

This time, Brian dribbled out of the wing, beating opponent after opponent. He centered the ball, and Justin bolted up just in time to kick it toward the goal. It was caught by the goalie. The goalie threw the ball back into play.

The opponents now had possession of the ball. They flew past the first defender, took a shot at the goal, and missed. "Make this one count!" bellowed the goalie as he kicked the ball out to his team.

Brian was determined to score. The game was nearly over, but there was still no score on the board. He raced down the field. He could hear the fans in the background. "Go! Score!" they roared.

In a last effort, the whole team charged down to help him out. They passed the ball around the opponents and worked closer and closer to the goal. Justin passed the ball to Brian, who took aim at the goal and gave it a mighty kick. The shot was good! The team had won!

"Congratulations! You guys were great! What a game!" cheered the coach.

1. Fill in the blanks with homophones. Justin was __one__ of the most determined players, so he was thrilled when his team __won__ the game.
2. Justin and Brian keep trying to make the goal. They are
   a. lazy.
   b. discouraged.
   (c. persistent.)
3. List all the words in this story that describe someone moving quickly. __dashed, darted, sprinted, bolted, rushed, flew, raced, charged__
4. How many times do Justin and Brian team up to make the shot? __three__
5. Write a different ending to this story. __Answers will vary.__

Last-Minute Stardom

It was time for the play to begin, but the lead actress had not arrived. When the door opened, everyone looked up expecting to see Beth.

Day #1

1. What clues does the title give you about what will happen in this writing? __someone will step in for the star—last-minute stardom__
2. What kind of writing is this: **fiction** or **nonfiction**? __fiction__
3. What kind of fiction takes place in this story? __a play__
4. Use your own words to state the problem the first paragraph introduces. __Answers will vary but should say the lead actress is late for the play.__

"I hate to put a damper on things, but Beth has a fever and cannot possibly make it tonight," explained her mom.

"Well, I never put all my eggs in one basket," responded Ms. King. "Amanda has been our understudy for that part and knows it well. Amanda, put on Beth's costume."

Day #2

1. An idiom is an expression that means something different from what it actually says. List any idioms in this selection. __I never put all my eggs in one basket.__
2. How did Ms. King respond to the problem? __She told Amanda to get ready.__
3. Had Amanda worked hard as the understudy? __yes__
4. What clues from the paragraph helped you answer #3? __She knows the part well.__

Amanda was on cloud nine as she jumped off the stage after the performance and ran to where her family and friends were waiting at the back of the auditorium.

"You were terrific. You always were the apple of my eye," said Dad, as he gave Amanda a hug. Amanda was speechless as everyone complimented her.

Day #3

1. List any idioms in this selection. __on cloud nine, the apple of my eye.__
2. Was Amanda pleased with her performance? How do you know? __yes, because she jumped off the stage and ran to her family__
3. How did the "Last-Minute Stardom" happen? __Answers will vary; students infer that Amanda played the lead role and did well.__
4. Why do you think Amanda was speechless after the performance? __Answers will vary.__

Dad said, "It's raining cats and dogs outside. Grandpa, keep an eye on everyone while I run and get the car."

Finally Dad returned. "Sorry it took so long. The traffic is slower than molasses in January. I avoided an accident in the parking lot only by the skin of my teeth."

Day #4

1. List any idioms in this selection. __slower than molasses in January, by the skin of my teeth__
2. What members of Amanda's family were at the performance? __Dad, Grandpa, others not mentioned__
3. What lesson could you take away after reading this story? __Answers will vary; study your part!__
4. Write a lesson someone could learn from this story. __Answers will vary.__

Assessment

1. Does the title give any specific information about the subject of this piece? Is the title an idiom? __No. It probably is, but only by reading the story can we be sure.__

Lay It on the Line

We were having a good time in the school hallway when out of the clear blue sky Jana started up. I knew it! She just had to ask me about my trip to Jamaica. Oh shoot, she really had me over a barrel. Man! I wanted to fly the coop. You see, a couple days before, I had lied about going to Jamaica. Sure, Jana's been there, but not me! It seems I can't hold a candle to her when it comes to interesting vacations to brag about.

2. An idiom is an expression that means something different from what it actually says. Match the idioms in this paragraph with the literal meaning below.

am greatly inferior	I can't hold a candle to
without warning	out of the clear blue sky
escape	fly the coop
helpless; at a disadvantage	over a barrel

"Why, Dougie," Jana teased. "What's wrong? Cat got your tongue?" She smiled roguishly at me.

Boy, that girl sure hit the nail on the head with that question. And then she nagged me all day.

3. Write your own literal meaning for the two idioms in the section above. __cat got your tongue = you aren't talking   hit the nail on the head = she was correct__

I warned her to cool it. You can't imagine how angry she makes me. Shoot! She didn't listen though. She really had a one-track mind! I was a sitting duck to her digs and verbal jabs. Then she started bragging about all her trips around the world! And the rest of the class was all ears to anything she'd say. In a nutshell, that girl is and always will be too big for her britches.

4. How many sentences end with an exclamation point? What does that tell you about how the author feels? __four; he feels strongly about what he is writing__
5. What do you think is the real cause of Dougie's problem: his lie about going to Jamaica or Jana traveling around the world? Explain. __Answers will vary.__

Answer Key

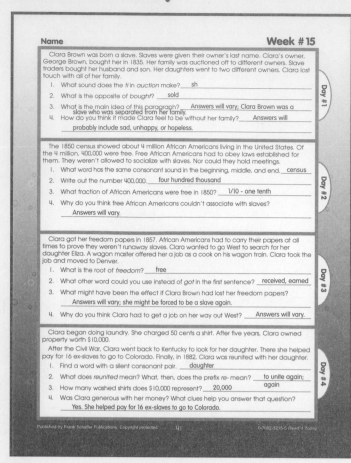

Week # 15

Name

Day #1

Clara Brown was born a slave. Slaves were given their owner's last name. Clara's owner, George Brown, bought her in 1835. Her family was auctioned off to different owners. Slave traders bought her husband and son. Her daughters went to two different owners. Clara lost touch with all of her family.

1. What sound does the *ti* in *auction* make? **sh**
2. What is the opposite of *bought*? **sold**
3. What is the main idea of this paragraph? **Answers will vary; Clara Brown was a slave who was separated from her family.**
4. How do you think it made Clara feel to be without her family? **Answers will probably include sad, unhappy, or hopeless.**

Day #2

The 1850 census showed about 4 million African Americans living in the United States. Of the 4 million, 400,000 were free. Free African Americans had to obey laws established for them. They weren't allowed to socialize with slaves. Nor could they hold meetings.

1. What word has the same consonant sound in the beginning, middle, and end. **census**
2. Write out the number 400,000. **four hundred thousand**
3. What fraction of African Americans were free in 1850? **1/10 - one tenth**
4. Why do you think free African Americans couldn't associate with slaves? **Answers will vary.**

Day #3

Clara got her freedom papers in 1857. African Americans had to carry their papers at all times to prove they weren't runaway slaves. Clara wanted to go West to search for her daughter Eliza. A wagon master offered her a job as a cook on his wagon train. Clara took the job and moved to Denver.

1. What is the root of *freedom*? **free**
2. What other word could you use instead of *got* in the first sentence? **received, earned**
3. What might have been the effect if Clara Brown had lost her freedom papers? **Answers will vary; she might be forced to be a slave again.**
4. Why do you think Clara had to get a job on her way out West? **Answers will vary.**

Day #4

Clara began doing laundry. She charged 50 cents a shirt. After five years, Clara owned property worth $10,000.

After the Civil War, Clara went back to Kentucky to look for her daughter. There she helped pay for 16 ex-slaves to go to Colorado. Finally, in 1882, Clara was reunited with her daughter.

1. Find a word with a silent consonant pair. **daughter**
2. What does *reunited* mean? What, then, does the prefix *re-* mean? **to unite again; again**
3. How many washed shirts does $10,000 represent? **20,000**
4. Was Clara generous with her money? What clues help you answer that question? **Yes. She helped pay for 16 ex-slaves to go to Colorado.**

Published by Frank Schaffer Publications. Copyright protected. 41   0-7682-3215-5 *Read 4 Today*

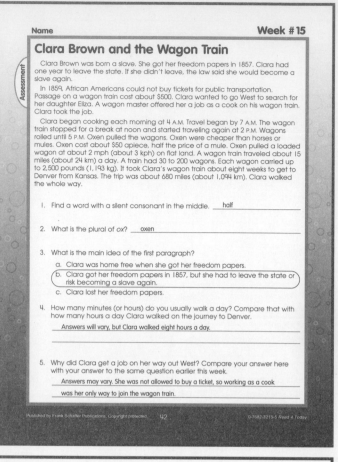

Week # 15

Name

Assessment

Clara Brown and the Wagon Train

Clara Brown was born a slave. She got her freedom papers in 1857. Clara had one year to leave the state. If she didn't leave, the law said she would become a slave again.

In 1859, African Americans could not buy tickets for public transportation. Passage on a wagon train cost about $500. Clara wanted to go West to search for her daughter Eliza. A wagon master offered her a job as a cook on his wagon train. Clara took the job.

Clara began cooking each morning at 4 A.M. Travel began by 7 A.M. The wagon train stopped for a break at noon and started traveling again at 2 P.M. Wagons rolled until 5 P.M. Oxen pulled the wagons. Oxen were cheaper than horses or mules. Oxen cost about $50 apiece, half the price of a mule. Oxen pulled a loaded wagon at about 2 mph (about 3 kph) on flat land. A wagon train traveled about 15 miles (about 24 km) a day. A train had 30 to 200 wagons. Each wagon carried up to 2,500 pounds (1,193 kg). It took Clara's wagon train about eight weeks to get to Denver from Kansas. The trip was about 680 miles (about 1,094 km). Clara walked the whole way.

1. Find a word with a silent consonant in the middle. **half**

2. What is the plural of *ox*? **oxen**

3. What is the main idea of the first paragraph?
   a. Clara was home free when she got her freedom papers.
   b. Clara got her freedom papers in 1857, but she had to leave the state or risk becoming a slave again.
   c. Clara lost her freedom papers.

4. How many minutes (or hours) do you usually walk a day? Compare that with how many hours a day Clara walked on the journey to Denver. **Answers will vary, but Clara walked eight hours a day.**

5. Why did Clara get a job on her way out West? Compare your answer here with your answer to the same question earlier this week. **Answers may vary. She was not allowed to buy a ticket, so working as a cook was her only way to join the wagon train.**

Published by Frank Schaffer Publications. Copyright protected. 42   0-7682-3215-5 *Read 4 Today*

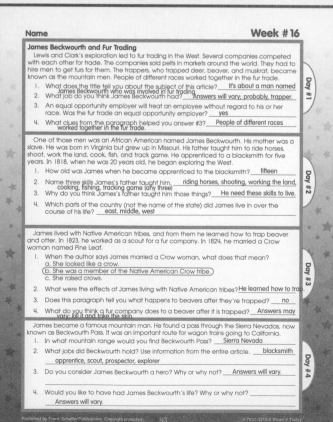

Week # 16

Name

Day #1

James Beckwourth and Fur Trading

Lewis and Clark's exploration led to fur trading in the West. Several companies competed with each other for trade. The companies sold pelts in markets around the world. They had to hire men to get furs for them. The trappers, who trapped deer, beaver, and muskrat, became known as the mountain men. People of different races worked together in the fur trade.

1. What does the title tell you about the subject of this article? **It's about a man named James Beckwourth who was involved in fur trading.**
2. What job do you think James Beckwourth had? **Answers will vary; probably, trapper.**
3. An equal opportunity employer will treat an employee without regard to his or her race. Was the fur trade an equal opportunity employer? **yes**
4. What clues from the paragraph helped you answer #3? **People of different races worked together in the fur trade.**

Day #2

One of those men was an African American named James Beckwourth. His mother was a slave. He was born in Virginia but grew up in Missouri. His father taught him to ride horses, shoot, work the land, cook, fish, and track game. He apprenticed to a blacksmith for five years. In 1818, when he was 20 years old, he began exploring the West.

1. How old was James when he became apprenticed to the blacksmith? **fifteen**
2. Name three skills James's father taught him. **riding horses, shooting, working the land, cooking, fishing, tracking game (any three)**
3. Why do you think James's father taught him those things? **He need these skills to live.**
4. Which parts of the country (not the name of the state) did James live in over the course of his life? **east, middle, west**

Day #3

James lived with Native American tribes, and from them he learned how to trap beaver and otter. In 1823, he worked as a scout for a fur company. In 1824, he married a Crow woman named Pine Leaf.

1. When the author says James married a Crow woman, what does that mean?
   a. She looked like a crow.
   b. She was a member of the Native American Crow tribe.
   c. She raised crows.
2. What were the effects of James living with Native American tribes? **He learned how to trap.**
3. Does this paragraph tell you what happens to beavers after they're trapped? **no**
4. What do you think a fur company does to a beaver after it is trapped? **Answers may vary; kill it and take the skin.**

Day #4

James became a famous mountain man. He found a pass through the Sierra Nevadas, now known as Beckwourth Pass. It was an important route for wagon trains going to California.

1. In what mountain range would you find Beckwourth Pass? **Sierra Nevada**
2. What jobs did Beckwourth hold? Use information from the entire article. **blacksmith apprentice, scout, prospector, explorer**
3. Do you consider James Beckwourth a hero? Why or why not? **Answers will vary.**
4. Would you like to have had James Beckwourth's life? Why or why not? **Answers will vary.**

Published by Frank Schaffer Publications. Copyright protected. 43   0-7682-3215-5 *Read 4 Today*

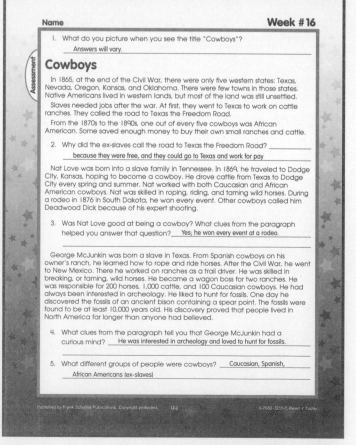

Week # 16

Name

Assessment

1. What do you picture when you see the title "Cowboys"? **Answers will vary.**

Cowboys

In 1865, at the end of the Civil War, there were only five western states: Texas, Nevada, Oregon, Kansas, and Oklahoma. There were few towns in those states. Native Americans lived in western lands, but most of the land was still unsettled.

Slaves needed jobs after the war. At first, they went to Texas to work on cattle ranches. They called the road to Texas the Freedom Road.

From the 1870s to the 1890s, one out of every five cowboys was African American. Some saved enough money to buy their own small ranches and cattle.

2. Why did the ex-slaves call the road to Texas the Freedom Road? **because they were free, and they could go to Texas and work for pay**

Nat Love was born into a slave family in Tennessee. In 1869, he traveled to Dodge City, Kansas, hoping to become a cowboy. He drove cattle from Texas to Dodge City every spring and summer. Nat worked with both Caucasian and African American cowboys. Nat was skilled in roping, riding, and taming wild horses. During a rodeo in 1876 in South Dakota, he won every event. Other cowboys called him Deadwood Dick because of his expert shooting.

3. Was Nat Love good at being a cowboy? What clues from the paragraph helped you answer that question? **Yes; he won every event at a rodeo.**

George McJunkin was born a slave in Texas. From Spanish cowboys on his owner's ranch, he learned how to rope and ride horses. After the Civil War, he went to New Mexico. There he worked on ranches as a trail rider. He was skilled in breaking, or taming, wild horses. He became a wagon boss for two ranches. He was responsible for 200 horses, 1,000 cattle, and 100 Caucasian cowboys. He had always been interested in archeology. He liked to hunt for fossils. One day he discovered the fossils of an ancient bison containing a spear point. The fossils were found to be at least 10,000 years old. His discovery proved that people lived in North America far longer than anyone had believed.

4. What clues from the paragraph tell you that George McJunkin had a curious mind? **He was interested in archeology and loved to hunt for fossils.**

5. What different groups of people were cowboys? **Caucasian, Spanish, African Americans (ex-slaves)**

Published by Frank Schaffer Publications. Copyright protected. 44   0-7682-3215-5 *Read 4 Today*

Answer Key

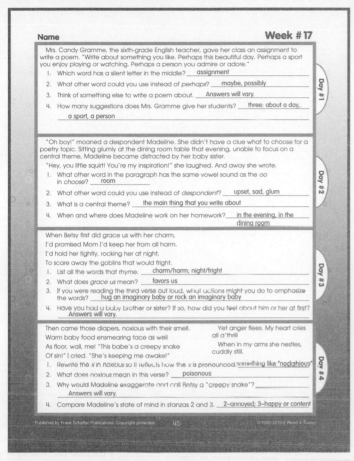

Name   **Week # 17**

Mrs. Candy Gramme, the sixth-grade English teacher, gave her class an assignment to write a poem. "Write about something you like. Perhaps this beautiful day. Perhaps a sport you enjoy playing or watching. Perhaps a person you admire or adore."

Day #1

1. Which word has a silent letter in the middle? __assignment__
2. What other word could you use instead of *perhaps*? __maybe, possibly__
3. Think of something else to write a poem about. __Answers will vary.__
4. How many suggestions does Mrs. Gramme give her students? __three: about a day, a sport, a person__

"Oh boy!" moaned a despondent Madeline. She didn't have a clue what to choose for a poetry topic. Sitting glumly at the dining room table that evening, unable to focus on a central theme, Madeline became distracted by her baby sister.

"Hey, you little squirt! You're my inspiration!" she laughed. And away she wrote.

Day #2

1. What other word in the paragraph has the same vowel sound as the *oo* in *choose*? __room__
2. What other word could you use instead of *despondent*? __upset, sad, glum__
3. What is a central theme? __the main thing that you write about__
4. When and where does Madeline work on her homework? __in the evening, in the dining room__

When Betsy first did grace us with her charm,
I'd promised Mom I'd keep her from all harm.
I'd hold her tightly, rocking her at night,
To scare away the goblins that would fright.

Day #3

1. List all the words that rhyme. __charm/harm; night/fright__
2. What does *grace us* mean? __favors us__
3. If you were reading the third verse out loud, what actions might you do to emphasize the words? __hug an imaginary baby or rock an imaginary baby__
4. Have you had a baby brother or sister? If so, how did you feel about him or her at first? __Answers will vary.__

Then came those diapers, noxious with their smell.
Warm baby food ensmearing face as well
As floor, wall, me! "This babe's a creepy snake
Of sin!" I cried. "She's keeping me awake!"

Yet anger flees. My heart cries all a'thrill
When in my arms she nestles, cuddly still.

Day #4

1. Rewrite the *x* in *noxious* so it reflects how the *x* is pronounced. __something like "nockshious"__
2. What does *noxious* mean in this verse? __poisonous__
3. Why would Madeline exaggerate and call Betsy a "creepy snake"? __Answers will vary.__
4. Compare Madeline's state of mind in stanzas 2 and 3. __2–annoyed; 3–happy or content__

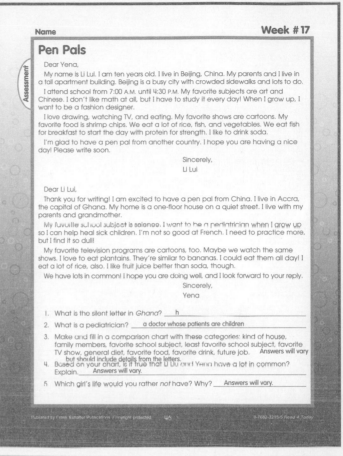

Name   **Week # 17**

Assessment

Pen Pals

Dear Yena,

My name is Li Lui. I am ten years old. I live in Beijing, China. My parents and I live in a tall apartment building. Beijing is a busy city with crowded sidewalks and lots to do.

I attend school from 7:00 A.M. until 4:30 P.M. My favorite subjects are art and Chinese. I don't like math at all, but I have to study it every day! When I grow up, I want to be a fashion designer.

I love drawing, watching TV, and eating. My favorite shows are cartoons. My favorite food is shrimp chips. We eat a lot of rice, fish, and vegetables. We eat fish for breakfast to start the day with protein for strength. I like to drink soda.

I'm glad to have a pen pal from another country. I hope you are having a nice day! Please write soon.

Sincerely,
Li Lui

Dear Li Lui,

Thank you for writing! I am excited to have a pen pal from China. I live in Accra, the capital of Ghana. My home is a one-floor house on a quiet street. I live with my parents and grandmother.

My favorite school subject is science. I want to be a pediatrician when I grow up so I can help heal sick children. I'm not so good at French. I need to practice more, but I find it so dull!

My favorite television programs are cartoons, too. Maybe we watch the same shows. I love to eat plantains. They're similar to bananas. I could eat them all day! I eat a lot of rice, also. I like fruit juice better than soda, though.

We have lots in common! I hope you are doing well, and I look forward to your reply.

Sincerely,
Yena

1. What is the silent letter in *Ghana*? __h__
2. What is a pediatrician? __a doctor whose patients are children__
3. Make and fill in a comparison chart with these categories: kind of house, family members, favorite school subject, least favorite school subject, favorite TV show, general diet, favorite food, favorite drink, future job. __Answers will vary but should include details from the letters.__
4. Based on your chart, is it true that Li Lui and Yena have a lot in common? Explain. __Answers will vary.__
5. Which girl's life would you rather *not* have? Why? __Answers will vary.__

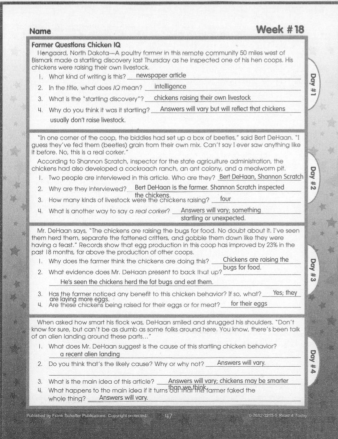

Name   **Week # 18**

Farmer Questions Chicken IQ

Hengaard, North Dakota—A poultry farmer in this remote community 50 miles west of Bismark made a startling discovery last Thursday as he inspected one of his hen coops. His chickens were raising their own livestock.

Day #1

1. What kind of writing is this? __newspaper article__
2. In the title, what does *IQ* mean? __intelligence__
3. What is the "startling discovery"? __chickens raising their own livestock__
4. Why do you think it was it startling? __Answers will vary but will reflect that chickens usually don't raise livestock.__

"In one corner of the coop, the biddies had set up a box of beetles," said Bert DeHaan. "I guess they've fed them (beetles) grain from their own mix. Can't say I ever saw anything like it before. No, this is a real corker."

According to Shannon Scratch, inspector for the state agriculture administration, the chickens had also developed a cockroach ranch, an ant colony, and a mealworm pit.

Day #2

1. Two people are interviewed in this article. Who are they? __Bert DeHaan, Shannon Scratch__
2. Why are they interviewed? __Bert DeHaan is the farmer. Shannon Scratch inspected the chickens.__
3. How many kinds of livestock were the chickens raising? __four__
4. What is another way to say a *real corker*? __Answers will vary; something startling or unexpected.__

Mr. DeHaan says, "The chickens are raising the bugs for food. No doubt about it. I've seen them herd them, separate the fattened critters, and gobble them down like they were having a feast." Records show that egg production in this coop has improved by 23% in the past 18 months, far above the production of other coops.

Day #3

1. Why does the farmer think the chickens are doing this? __Chickens are raising the bugs for food.__
2. What evidence does Mr. DeHaan present to back that up? __He's seen the chickens herd the fat bugs and eat them.__
3. Has the farmer noticed any benefit to this chicken behavior? If so, what? __Yes; they are laying more eggs.__
4. Are these chickens being raised for their eggs or for meat? __for their eggs__

When asked how smart his flock was, DeHaan smiled and shrugged his shoulders. "Don't know for sure, but can't be as dumb as some folks around here. You know, there's been talk of an alien landing around these parts..."

Day #4

1. What does Mr. DeHaan suggest is the cause of this startling chicken behavior? __a recent alien landing__
2. Do you think that's the likely cause? Why or why not? __Answers will vary.__
3. What is the main idea of this article? __Answers will vary; chickens may be smarter than we think.__
4. What happens to the main idea if it turns out that the farmer faked the whole thing? __Answers will vary.__

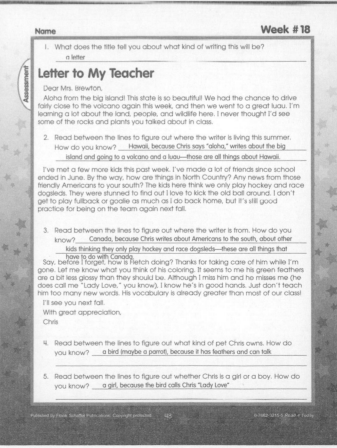

Name   **Week # 18**

Assessment

1. What does the title tell you about what kind of writing this will be? __a letter__

Letter to My Teacher

Dear Mrs. Brewton,

Aloha from the big island! This state is so beautiful! We had the chance to drive fairly close to the volcano again this week, and then we went to a great luau. I'm learning a lot about the land, people, and wildlife here. I never thought I'd see some of the rocks and plants you talked about in class.

2. Read between the lines to figure out where the writer is living this summer. How do you know? __Hawaii, because Chris says "aloha," writes about the big island and going to a volcano and a luau—those are all things about Hawaii.__

I've met a few more kids this past week. I've made a lot of friends since school ended in June. By the way, how are things in North Country? Any news from those friendly Americans to your south? The kids here think we only play hockey and race dogsleds. They were stunned to find out I love to kick the old ball around. I don't get to play fullback or goalie as much as I do back home, but it's still good practice for being on the team again next fall.

3. Read between the lines to figure out where the writer is from. How do you know? __Canada, because Chris writes about Americans to the south, about other kids thinking they only play hockey and race dogsleds—these are all things that have to do with Canada.__

Say, before I forget, how is Fletch doing? Thanks for taking care of him while I'm gone. Let me know what you think of his coloring. It seems to me his green feathers are a bit less glossy than they should be. Although I miss him and he misses me (he does call me "Lady Love," you know), I know he's in good hands. Just don't teach him too many new words. His vocabulary is already greater than most of our class!

I'll see you next fall.

With great appreciation,
Chris

4. Read between the lines to figure out what kind of pet Chris owns. How do you know? __a bird (maybe a parrot), because it has feathers and can talk__

5. Read between the lines to figure out whether Chris is a girl or a boy. How do you know? __a girl, because the bird calls Chris "Lady Love"__

Answer Key

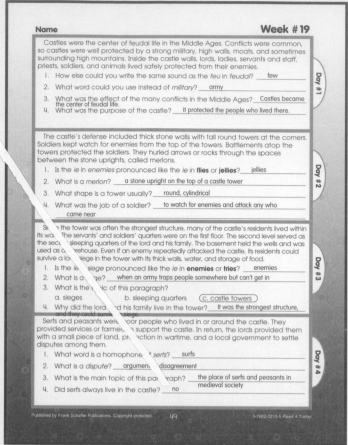

Name   **Week #19**

Castles were the center of feudal life in the Middle Ages. Conflicts were common, so castles were well protected by a strong military, high walls, moats, and sometimes surrounding high mountains. Inside the castle walls, lords, ladies, servants and staff, priests, soldiers, and animals lived safely protected from their enemies.

Day #1

1. How else could you write the same sound as the *feu* in *feudal*? ___few___
2. What word could you use instead of *military*? ___army___
3. What was the effect of the many conflicts in the Middle Ages? ___Castles became the center of feudal life.___
4. What was the purpose of the castle? ___It protected the people who lived there.___

The castle's defense included thick stone walls with tall round towers at the corners. Soldiers kept watch for enemies from the top of the towers. Battlements atop the towers protected the soldiers. They hurled arrows or rocks through the spaces between the stone uprights, called merlons.

Day #2

1. Is the *ie* in *enemies* pronounced like the *ie* in **flies** or **jellies**? ___jellies___
2. What is a *merlon*? ___a stone upright on the top of a castle tower___
3. What shape is a tower usually? ___round, cylindrical___
4. What was the job of a soldier? ___to watch for enemies and attack any who came near___

Si___ the tower was often the strongest structure, many of the castle's residents lived within its wa___. The servants' and soldiers' quarters were on the first floor. The second level served as the sec___ sleeping quarters of the lord and his family. The basement held the wells and was used as a ___rehouse. Even if an enemy repeatedly attacked the castle, its residents could survive a lo___ siege in the tower with its thick walls, water, and storage of food.

Day #3

1. Is the *ie* in *siege* pronounced like the *ie* in **enemies** or **tries**? ___enemies___
2. What is a ___ge? ___when an army traps people somewhere but can't get in___
3. What is the ___ic of this paragraph?
   a. sieges   b. sleeping quarters   (c. castle towers)
4. Why did the lord ___d his family live in the tower? ___It was the strongest structure, and they could survi___ siege.___

Serfs and peasants were ___oor people who lived in or around the castle. They provided services or farmed ___o support the castle. In return, the lords provided them with a small piece of land, pr___ction in wartime, and a local government to settle disputes among them.

Day #4

1. What word is a homophone ___ *serfs*? ___surfs___
2. What is a *dispute*? ___argument, disagreement___
3. What is the main topic of this pa___raph? ___the place of serfs and peasants in medieval society___
4. Did serfs always live in the castle? ___no___

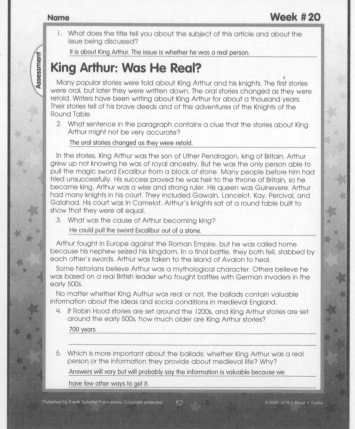

Name   **Week #19**

Castle Days

Assessment

Knights and soldiers were trained warriors who were given land in exchange for protection of the castle. Knights and their horses dressed in heavy, protective armor made of iron. When they were not in battles, jousting kept them active. Jousting was a combat between two armed knights on horses carrying lances.

The rulers were wealthy lords and ladies, or royalty, who built the castle to defend their land. They were expected to treat soldiers and those who served them with honor. Lords often acted as judges and presided over the feudal court under strict codes of behavior. Life in a castle could be exciting for its rulers.

The castle social life revolved around the great hall. It contained the kitchen, chapel, and garderobes (toilets), with a huge warming fire in the center. Fancy medieval feasts were celebrated here. Lords and ladies danced and listened to minstrels. On special occasions, entertainment included a joust.

Only a few castles containing the relics of medieval days stand intact. However, the ruins of many castles can still be found in Europe. Suits of armor, authentic weapons, and beautiful castle tapestries are displayed in museums around the world today.

1. Which letters are silent in *knights*? ___k, g, h___

2. What is jousting? ___a pretend battle between two knights who ride horses while carrying lances___

3. Use one to three words each to describe the main topic for each of the four paragraphs.
   ___1 – knights and soldiers; 2 – rulers; 3 – the great hall/castle social life___

4. What are the two purposes of a joust? ___practice for the knights and entertainment for the lords and ladies___

5. Compare a medieval feast with your idea of a great feast. ___Answers will vary.___

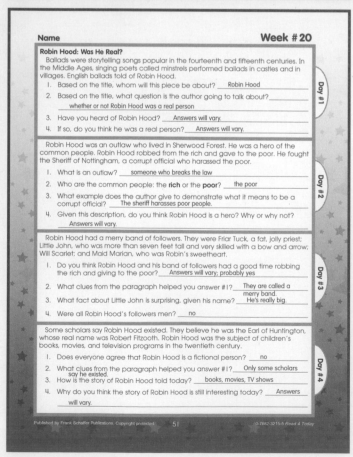

Name   **Week #20**

Robin Hood: Was He Real?

Ballads were storytelling songs popular in the fourteenth and fifteenth centuries. In the Middle Ages, singing poets called minstrels performed ballads in castles and in villages. English ballads told of Robin Hood.

Day #1

1. Based on the title, whom will this piece be about? ___Robin Hood___
2. Based on the title, what question is the author going to talk about? ___whether or not Robin Hood was a real person___
3. Have you heard of Robin Hood? ___Answers will vary.___
4. If so, do you think he was a real person? ___Answers will vary.___

Robin Hood was an outlaw who lived in Sherwood Forest. He was a hero of the common people. Robin Hood robbed from the rich and gave to the poor. He fought the Sheriff of Nottingham, a corrupt official who harassed the poor.

Day #2

1. What is an outlaw? ___someone who breaks the law___
2. Who are the common people: the **rich** or the **poor**? ___the poor___
3. What example does the author give to demonstrate what it means to be a corrupt official? ___The sheriff harasses poor people.___
4. Given this description, do you think Robin Hood is a hero? Why or why not? ___Answers will vary.___

Robin Hood had a merry band of followers. They were Friar Tuck, a fat, jolly priest; Little John, who was more than seven feet tall and very skilled with a bow and arrow; Will Scarlet; and Maid Marian, who was Robin's sweetheart.

Day #3

1. Do you think Robin Hood and his band of followers had a good time robbing the rich and giving to the poor? ___Answers will vary; probably yes___
2. What clues from the paragraph helped you answer #1? ___They are called a merry band.___
3. What fact about Little John is surprising, given his name? ___He's really big.___
4. Were all Robin Hood's followers men? ___no___

Some scholars say Robin Hood existed. They believe he was the Earl of Huntington, whose real name was Robert Fitzooth. Robin Hood was the subject of children's books, movies, and television programs in the twentieth century.

Day #4

1. Does everyone agree that Robin Hood is a fictional person? ___no___
2. What clues from the paragraph helped you answer #1? ___Only some scholars say he existed.___
3. How is the story of Robin Hood told today? ___books, movies, TV shows___
4. Why do you think the story of Robin Hood is still interesting today? ___Answers will vary.___

Name   **Week #20**

Assessment

1. What does the title tell you about the subject of this article and about the issue being discussed? ___It is about King Arthur. The issue is whether he was a real person.___

King Arthur: Was He Real?

Many popular stories were told about King Arthur and his knights. The first stories were oral, but later they were written down. The oral stories changed as they were retold. Writers have been writing about King Arthur for about a thousand years. Their stories tell of his brave deeds and of the adventures of the Knights of the Round Table.

2. What sentence in the paragraph contains a clue that the stories about King Arthur might not be very accurate? ___The oral stories changed as they were retold.___

In the stories, King Arthur was the son of Uther Pendragon, king of Britain. Arthur grew up not knowing he was of royal ancestry. But he was the only person able to pull the magic sword Excalibur from a block of stone. Many people before him had tried unsuccessfully. His success proved he was heir to the throne of Britain, so he became king. Arthur was a wise and strong ruler. His queen was Guinevere. Arthur had many knights in his court. They included Gawain, Lancelot, Kay, Percival, and Galahad. His court was in Camelot. Arthur's knights sat at a round table built to show that they were all equal.

3. What was the cause of Arthur becoming king? ___He could pull the sword Excalibur out of a stone.___

Arthur fought in Europe against the Roman Empire, but he was called home because his nephew seized his kingdom. In a final battle, they both fell, stabbed by each other's swords. Arthur was taken to the island of Avalon to heal.

Some historians believe Arthur was a mythological character. Others believe he was based on a real British leader who fought battles with German invaders in the early 500s.

No matter whether King Authur was real or not, the ballads contain valuable information about the ideas and social conditions in medieval England.

4. If Robin Hood stories are set around the 1200s, and King Arthur stories are set around the early 500s, how much older are King Arthur stories? ___700 years___

5. Which is more important about the ballads: whether King Arthur was a real person or the information they provide about medieval life? Why? ___Answers will vary but will probably say the information is valuable because we have few other ways to get it.___

Answer Key

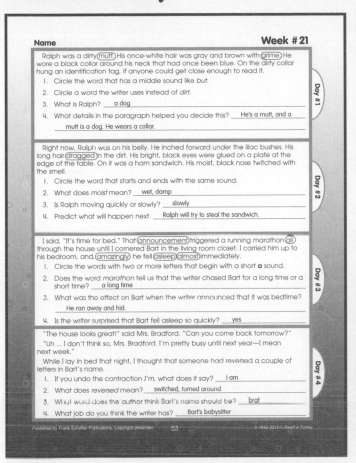

Name   **Week # 21**

Ralph was a dirty (mutt). His once-white hair was gray and brown with (grime). He wore a black collar around his neck that had once been blue. On the dirty collar hung an identification tag, if anyone could get close enough to read it.

1. Circle a word that has a middle sound like *but*.
2. Circle a word the writer uses instead of *dirt*.
3. What is Ralph? __a dog__
4. What details in the paragraph helped you decide this? __He's a mutt, and a__ __mutt is a dog. He wears a collar.__

Day #1

Right now, Ralph was on his belly. He inched forward under the lilac bushes. His long hair (dragged) in the dirt. His bright, black eyes were glued on a plate at the edge of the table. On it was a ham sandwich. His moist, black nose twitched with the smell.

1. Circle the word that starts and ends with the same sound.
2. What does *moist* mean? __wet, damp__
3. Is Ralph moving quickly or slowly? __slowly__
4. Predict what will happen next. __Ralph will try to steal the sandwich.__

Day #2

I said, "It's time for bed." That (announcement) triggered a running marathon (all) through the house until I cornered Bart in the living room closet. I carried him up to his bedroom, and, (amazingly) he fell (asleep) (almost) immediately.

1. Circle the words with two or more letters that begin with a short **a** sound.
2. Does the word *marathon* tell us that the writer chased Bart for a long time or a short time? __a long time__
3. What was the effect on Bart when the writer announced that it was bedtime? __He ran away and hid.__
4. Is the writer surprised that Bart fell asleep so quickly? __yes__

Day #3

"The house looks great!" said Mrs. Bradford. "Can you come back tomorrow?"
"Uh … I don't think so, Mrs. Bradford. I'm pretty busy until next year—I mean next week."
While I lay in bed that night, I thought that someone had reversed a couple of letters in Bart's name.

1. If you undo the contraction *I'm*, what does it say? __I am__
2. What does *reversed* mean? __switched, turned around__
3. What word does the author think Bart's name should be? __brat__
4. What job do you think the writer has? __Bart's babysitter__

Day #4

Name   **Week # 21**

Assessment

Summer Storm

Brian went zooming to the park on his bike. It started out as a perfect day, until Brian's mom made him drag his little brother Pete along.

"Wait for me, Brian," whined Pete as he tried to keep up.

Brian parked his bike and followed his nose to the concession stand. There were sizzling burgers on the grill, fresh-popped popcorn, and big barrels of fizzing root beer. He made his purchase and handed Pete his lunch. "Sit here and eat, and don't move until I come back to get you," Brian said.

As Pete began eating, he heard the pitter-patter of rain falling around him, but he stayed dry under the large tree. As the rain increased, the wind began to howl. With the leaves rustling above his head, it sounded as though it was raining harder. Then he heard the plink of the hail on the roof of the concession stand. When Pete saw lightning in the distance, he knew he should move from under the tree. Brian would just have to look for him.

When the storm got worse, Brian knew he had to find Pete. Brian thought he heard his name as he ran but then wondered if it was the wind playing tricks on him. There it was again. "Brian!" That voice had never sounded so good.

1. Find a word that has two c's in it, each pronounced a different way.
   __concession__
2. What happened to the rain when it increased? __It rained more and harder.__
3. This story is full of words whose sounds make you think of what they mean, such as zooming and fizzing. Words like these are examples of onomatopoeia. Use the clues to write the correct word from the story on the line. Each word will be an example of onomatopoeia.
   a. moving rapidly __zooming__
   b. sharp, metallic sound __plink__
   c. a series of light, quick, tapping sounds __pitter-patter__
4. Write clues for two other examples of onomatopoeia used in the story.
   __Answers will vary.__
5. Why was it a good decision for Pete to leave the tree during the lightning storm?
   __Lightning hits trees, and Pete could have been hurt if he had stayed under the tree.__

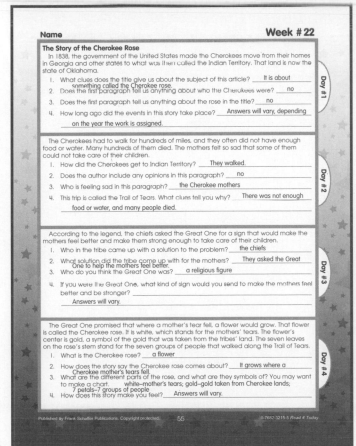

Name   **Week # 22**

The Story of the Cherokee Rose
In 1838, the government of the United States made the Cherokees move from their homes in Georgia and other states to what was then called the Indian Territory. That land is now the state of Oklahoma.

1. What clues does the title give us about the subject of this article? __It is about__ __something called the Cherokee rose.__
2. Does the first paragraph tell us anything about who the Cherokees were? __no__
3. Does the first paragraph tell us anything about the rose in the title? __no__
4. How long ago did the events in this story take place? __Answers will vary, depending__ __on the year the work is assigned.__

Day #1

The Cherokees had to walk for hundreds of miles, and they often did not have enough food or water. Many hundreds of them died. The mothers felt so sad that some of them could not take care of their children.

1. How did the Cherokees get to Indian Territory? __They walked.__
2. Does the author include any opinions in this paragraph? __no__
3. Who is feeling sad in this paragraph? __the Cherokee mothers__
4. This trip is called the Trail of Tears. What clues tell you why? __There was not enough__ __food or water, and many people died.__

Day #2

According to the legend, the chiefs asked the Great One for a sign that would make the mothers feel better and make them strong enough to take care of their children.

1. Who in the tribe came up with a solution to the problem? __the chiefs__
2. What solution did the tribe come up with for the mothers? __They asked the Great__ __One to help the mothers feel better.__
3. Who do you think the Great One was? __a religious figure__
4. If you were the Great One, what kind of sign would you send to make the mothers feel better and be stronger? _____
   __Answers will vary.__

Day #3

The Great One promised that where a mother's tear fell, a flower would grow. That flower is called the Cherokee rose. It is white, which stands for the mothers' tears. The flower's center is gold, a symbol of the gold that was taken from the tribes' land. The seven leaves on the rose's stem stand for the seven groups of people that walked along the Trail of Tears.

1. What is the Cherokee rose? __a flower__
2. How does the story say the Cherokee rose comes about? __It grows where a__ __Cherokee mother's tears fell.__
3. What are the different parts of the rose, and what are they symbols of? You may want to make a chart. __white–mother's tears; gold–gold taken from Cherokee lands;__ __7 petals–7 groups of people__
4. How does this story make you feel? __Answers will vary.__

Day #4

Name   **Week # 22**

Assessment

1. Without looking back on your earlier work, what do you remember about the Trail of Tears? __Answers will vary.__

The Trail of Tears

The ancient Cherokee were hunters and farmers. They lived in the area that we know as the Appalachian Mountains of Georgia. But in 1829, white settlers found gold on this land. They went to the United States government and asked that the Cherokee be forced to leave the land, hoping they would then get the rights to it.

2. Why did the settlers want the Cherokee to leave? __The settlers wanted__ __the gold found on the Cherokees' land.__

A new law called the Indian Removal Act of 1830 was passed. The law stated that all Native Americans east of the Mississippi would be moved. They would have to move to an Indian territory in the west, an area in what is now Oklahoma.

3. Were the settlers successful? __yes__

Some agreed to go, but most would not leave their land. Starting in the spring of 1838, the army gathered the Cherokee together. The people were held in forts like prisoners. Within one month, the first group of Cherokee was forced to leave Georgia. They marched over 1,000 miles to the new land. Some people had horses and wagons. Most people walked. The trip lasted many months. Thousands died, either during the march or once they got to the land. There was no shelter or food at the territory. The last group of Cherokee arrived on the Indian Territory in March of 1839. In all, almost 17,000 Cherokee were forced to move to the new land.

4. Did the Cherokee go willingly? __no__
5. Do you think it was a fair trade: thousands of dead and displaced Cherokees for a chance to mine gold? Why or why not?
   __Answers will vary.__

Answer Key

Week # 23 (page 57)

Name _____ **Week # 23**

Each year, the citizens of the United States celebrate two holidays to remember servicemen and women who fought in wars to preserve citizens' freedom. On November 11, Veterans Day is celebrated, and on the last Monday in May, Memorial Day is celebrated.

Day #1

1. What is the silent consonant pair in this paragraph? __gh__
2. What is a synonym for *celebrated* as it is used here: **partied** or **observed**? __observed__
3. Which sentence is the topic sentence? __the first sentence__
4. Which holiday has a date that is relative (the date we observe it depends on another factor)? __Memorial Day__

On November 11, 1918, a treaty was signed between the Germans and the Allied forces of the United States, France, Great Britain, Russia, and Italy, putting an end to World War I. It was first called Armistice Day, but it is now called Veterans Day. George Honey, an Australian journalist, asked the whole world to remain silent for two minutes as the treaty was signed. Even the radios were silent.

Day #2

1. How do you pronounce the *ss* in *Russia*? __sh__
2. What does *armistice* mean?
   a. beginning of war   b. declaration of the winner of the battle   (c. parties agree to end war)
3. If you read the second sentence of this paragraph out loud, which two words would you emphasize? __first, now__
4. Can one person make a difference in how the whole world behaves? What details from the paragraph helped you answer that question? __Yes; George Honey got worldwide silence for two minutes.__

Memorial Day began after the Civil War, when people began decorating the graves of soldiers who had died in the war. Although many claim to have started the tradition, Congress declared Waterloo, New York, the birthplace of Memorial Day when the whole community held a celebration on May 5, 1866.

Day #3

1. Find a compound word in this paragraph. __birthplace__
2. What is a grave? __a place where a body is buried__
3. Which holiday is older: **Memorial Day** or **Veterans Day**? __Memorial Day__
4. How many years older is that holiday? __52 years__

In 1868, the Grand Army of the Republic organized a ceremony at the National Cemetery in Arlington, Virginia. They called it Decoration Day because they decorated the graves of soldiers. The holiday stuck, but the name was changed to Memorial Day. On this day, many communities hold parades in remembrance of servicemen and women who gave their lives for the freedom of the United States.

Day #4

1. Find an example of alliteration in this paragraph. __Decoration Day__
2. What word is the opposite of *freedom*? __slavery__
3. Restate the last sentence in your own words. __Answers will vary.__
4. Do you think we should combine the two holidays into one? Why or why not? __Answers will vary.__

Week # 23 (page 58)

Name _____ **Week # 23**

Assessment

The Statue of Liberty

The Statue of Liberty is a symbol of freedom and welcome to the world. Frédéric Bartholdi of France sculpted the statue. It was a gift from France to the United States. The statue symbolized friendship between the two countries. It was also intended to honor the birthday of the United States' independence. President Grover Cleveland dedicated the statue in 1886. It became a national monument in 1924. The statue is located on Liberty Island in New York Harbor.

The original name for the statue was "Liberty Enlightening the World." The statue's torch is a welcome symbol to immigrants. It's Liberty's way of enlightening the world. The crown has seven rays. They symbolize the seven oceans and the seven continents. Liberty has a tablet in her left hand. It shows the date July 4, 1776. The broken chain at her feet symbolizes freedom. Her Greek robe symbolizes Greece as the birthplace of democracy.

Liberty stands on a pedestal. Americans had to raise money to pay for the pedestal. Joseph Pulitzer was editor of *The World*, a New York newspaper. He thought the statue was a great idea. His newspaper ran articles about raising money for the statue. He published the names of people who gave money. He even listed the names of children who sent pennies. Americans raised $250,000. That was enough money to pay for the pedestal. The French people paid for the statue.

1. What are the prefix, root, and suffix in *Enlightening*? __prefix – en; root – light; suffix – ening__

2. What is a symbol?
   (a. an image that stands for an idea)
   b. a part of a drum kit
   c. a statue

3. What is the main idea of paragraph 2? __Answers will vary but will probably focus on what the different parts of the statue symbolize.__

4. What is the symbol for the oceans and continents? __the seven rays of the crown__

5. Imagine you were a kid in the 1880s. Do you think you would've sent in pennies to pay for the pedestal? Why or why not? __Answers will vary.__

Week # 24 (page 59)

Name _____ **Week # 24**

Slumber Party

It was the night Annabel had looked forward to for weeks! Four girls were arriving for a sleepover party. Finally, four cars pulled up and the doorbell rang. Annabel threw open the door and welcomed her guests. The girls piled into Annabel's house in a jumble of sleeping bags and overnight cases.

Day #1

1. What clues does the title give you about the subject of this story? __It is about a slumber party.__
2. What is another way to say *slumber party*? __a sleepover__
3. Do you imagine that kids get a lot of sleep at a slumber party? __Answers may vary; probably no__
4. How many girls in all are at the party? __five__

Thank you for inviting me," Robin replied. "I brought you a thank-you gift." She held out a small box to her hostess.

"Yum! Chocolates!" Sheila shouted. She grabbed the box and shoved a candy into her mouth. She dropped the empty wrapper on the floor. "Got any milk?" she said, her mouth full.

Day #2

1. Which word describes Robin?   a. fearful   b. greedy   (c. polite)
2. Write two examples of Robin's behavior from the story to prove why your description fits. __She says thank you right away and brings a gift.__
3. Which word describes Sheila?   (a. rude)   b. fearful   c. gracious
4. Write two examples of Sheila's behavior from the story to prove why your description fits. __She grabs the chocolate without asking and talks while she has food in her mouth.__

Annabel noticed that one of her guests did not look happy. "Tamiko, what's wrong?"
"I've never slept away from home," Tamiko admitted. "I'm a little nervous."
"You'll be all right," Annabel reassured her. "But, you can use the phone to call home if you need to. It's right over there . . . Hey? Where's the phone?"

Day #3

1. Which word describes Tamiko?   (a. fearful)   b. rude   c. greedy
2. Write two examples of Tamiko's behavior from the story to prove why your description fits. __She stands quietly and says she's nervous.__
3. What advice would you give Tamiko to help her get over her nervousness? __Answers will vary.__
4. Does this paragraph tell you anything about what time of year this story takes place? __no__

Paula had the phone. "Is it okay if Dan comes over?" She called to Annabel. "He is bored."
"No!" Annabel responded, a little shocked. "There are no boys at this slumber party."
"Oh." Paula rolled her eyes and went back to chatting on the phone.

Day #4

1. Which word describes Paula?   a. gracious   (b. rude)   c. polite
2. Write two examples of Paula's behavior from the story to prove why your description fits. __She takes the phone, asks for someone else to come over, and rolls her eyes.__
3. Compare each girl's behavior. What is the first thing each girl did after walking through the door? __Robin thanked Annabel, Sheila grabbed food, Tamiko stood quietly, Paula took the phone.__
4. Girls: Which kind of guest do you think you would be more like? Boys: If there were a girls' slumber party at your house, what would you do? __Answers will vary.__

Week # 24 (page 60)

Name _____ **Week # 24**

Assessment

1. What kind of writing will this be? __a journal__

Ben's Journal

February 9

Tomorrow is the big day. I've studied so hard for the past three weeks that I think I could spell these words in my sleep.

But what if I get nervous and mess up? What if someone else knows more words than I know? Rebecca always wins when we practice at school. I just want to do the best that I can.

Mom has helped me every night after supper. She says that studying and learning are more important, in the long run, than winning. I guess she's right. But I still really hope I win.

2. Circle the words that best describe how Ben was feeling the day before the event.
   (confident)   tired   (anxious)   happy

February 10

I did it! Well, I didn't win first place, but I came in second. And I'm really proud of that.

At first, I was scared when I looked out and saw all those people in the audience. I was afraid I'd forget everything. But then I told myself, "You studied hard. You know all those words. Come on, you can do it!"

3. What was Ben's strategy to getting over his nervousness? __He reminded himself that he's studied hard.__

My first word was *indicate*: i-n-d-i-c-a-t-e. It was easy. Then I knew I could do the rest of them, too. The only word that really stumped me was *cannibal*. I spelled it c-a-n-n-i-b-l-e—oops. Rebecca spelled it right, along with her last word: *hydraulics*.

Oh well, I won a dictionary and had my picture taken for the newspaper. When I came home, my family had a party to celebrate! Tomorrow, I start studying for next year's contest.

4. How did Ben feel about winning second place?
   a. upset because he didn't win first place
   (b. happy because he did his best)
   c. angry at the person who beat him

5. What do you think will happen next year at the spelling contest? Write a journal entry from Ben's point of view about what might happen. __Answers will vary.__

Answer Key

My favorite blood-pumping, wholly invigorating game was King of the Mountain. You see, one player would dash up the hillock, pose menacingly at the top, and claim, "King of the Mountain!" Then the attackers would pull, push, or tackle to dethrone the king. Whoever next reached the lofty heights would exclaim, "King of the Mountain!" And the game would start anew.

Day #1

1. Does the **c** in *menacingly* have the same beginning sound as **king** or **sing**? ___sing___
2. What is the prefix in *dethrone*? What does *dethrone* mean? ___de –; take someone off the throne___
3. There are some great adjectives in this paragraph. List them. ___blood-pumping, wholly invigorating, lofty___
4. Does this game sound like it has a lot of rules? ___no___

School teachers frowned on the game. And for good reason. Bloody noses, arguing combatants, torn clothing, and broken spectacles resulted in phone calls from concerned parents and, consequently, a new "Thou Shalt Not . . ." rule in the school playground rules book. No, school was no place for this sport.

Day #2

1. Does the first syllable of *combatants* sound more like **come** or **comb**? ___come___
2. What are combatants? ___people fighting against one another___
3. There is a chain of cause and effect in sentence 3 of this paragraph. Restate it briefly in your own words. ___kids get hurt, parents call the school to complain, kids aren't allowed to play the game at school___
4. Does the author agree with the school rule that they are not allowed to play King of the Mountain at school? ___yes___

So we played King of the Mountain after school hours on other turf. No supervision. Most parents averted their eyes, crossed their fingers, and prayed for swift healing for whatever injuries would surely occur. Pretty cool. Pretty naïve, too.

Day #3

1. How does the *i* in *naïve* sound: **ee** or **ay**? ___ee___
2. What does *naïve* mean?   a. full of fun   b. soft and squishy   (c. lacking in wisdom)
3. The author uses very short sentences to emphasize certain ideas. List them. ___No supervision. Pretty cool. Pretty naïve, too.___
4. How does the author feel about the parents who let their kids play King of the Mountain? ___The author likes them and thinks they're foolish.___

A youthful attacker, missing his target, slid over a snow mound and skidded into the path of a fast-approaching snowplow. Only because a fellow player grabbed him by the collar and yanked him into a ditch was a catastrophe avoided. The near-victim was so shaken that he remained in bed for a week.

Day #4

1. Do you pronounce the *e* in *catastrophe*? ___yes___
2. What is the suffix in *youthful*? What does *youthful* mean? ___– ful; full of youth, young___
3. If you read sentence 1 out loud, how would you read it to reflect the action it describes?   a. lazily   (b. quickly)   c. really loudly
4. Do the descriptions of the game make you want to play it or want to avoid it? Explain. ___Answers will vary.___

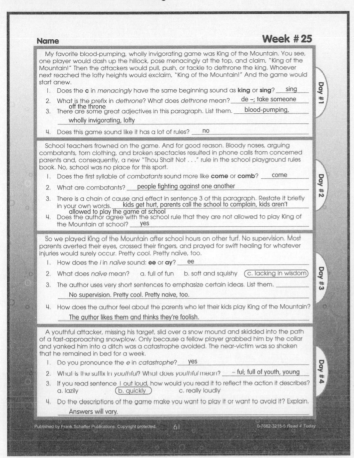

Save the Day

Assessment

Tate raced toward the baseball diamond. He greeted his teammates, jumping up and down. "Are you ready to win the championship?" he asked excitedly.

His two best friends, Jeffrey and Alyssa, smiled at his excitement. "It looks like our star batter is ready," Jeffrey said. Jeffrey didn't want to admit that he was pretty nervous. Lately, he'd been in a slump. His average had declined late in the season. He hoped he could pull it back up today when it counted most.

Alyssa was calm, as usual. She never seemed to get butterflies in her stomach, even under pressure. She was the team's pitcher and had a mean fastball.

The players warmed up and took the field. The game was a close one, but Tate and his team were victorious in the end. Afterward, the three buddies went to a nearby ice-cream shop to celebrate.

"Great job today, Alyssa!" Tate complimented his friend. "You kept your cool even when we were behind 2 to 0."

"Thanks," Alyssa said modestly. She licked her black raspberry cone neatly. Not a drip escaped off the cone.

"You were pretty great yourself," Jeffrey said to Tate. "I jumped off the bench, almost knocking it over, when you hit that ball over the fence in the fifth inning!" The two boys gave each other high fives. In their enthusiasm, the boys knocked Tate's ice cream off its cone.

"Oh, no," Tate said, disappointedly.

"Sorry, Tate," Jeffrey said. But Jeffrey couldn't stop smiling. He was in too good a mood. He'd hit the winning run today, and he felt great. He hadn't let his team down. Now, he wouldn't let his friend down.

"I have some money left," he said to Tate. "Let's go back up to the counter so I can save the day again!"

1. Find a word that has a *u* with an **oo** sound. ___enthusiasm___
2. What is a synonym for *celebrate* as it is used here? (party) or **observe**?
3. Compare how each kid feels before the game. ___Tate, excited; Jeffrey, nervous; Alyssa, calm___
4. The author tells you that Alyssa doesn't get too nervous. What actions of hers tell you that she doesn't get too excited either? ___She eats her ice cream neatly, and she talks modestly after the championship.___
5. Which kid is a bit of a klu___ ___do you know? ___Jeffrey, because he almost knocked over the bench and knocked Tate's ice cream off the cone.___

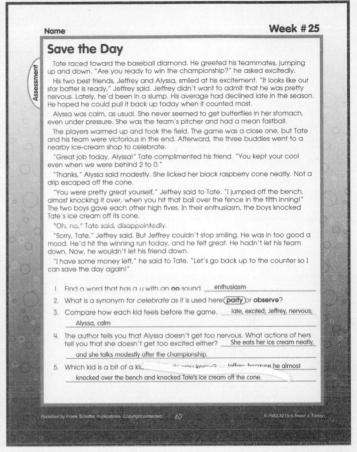

The Sydney Opera House

The Sydney Opera House is world-famous. It has an unusual design. It is one of the most unusual buildings in the world. The Opera House is Sydney's most famous landmark. It's located in Sydney Harbor.

Day #1

1. What clues does the title give you? ___It's about an opera house in Sydney.___
2. Does the first paragraph tell you where Sydney is? ___no___
3. Do you think the opera house is near water? ___yes___
4. What details from the paragraph helped you answer #3? ___A harbor is on the water, and the opera house is near the harbor.___

Danish architect Jørn Utson designed the Sydney Opera House. He won a contest for his design. Work began in 1959 and was completed in 1973. The estimate for the Sydney Opera House was $7 million (Australian). However, the final cost was $102 million.

Day #2

1. Does this paragraph give you a clue about where Sydney is? If so, where? ___yes; Australia___
2. How long did it take to build the Sydney Opera House? ___14 years___
3. How much over budget was the building? ___$95 million (Australian)___
4. Was the cost estimate very accurate? ___no___

Utson wanted the roof to look like sails on a giant sailing ship. Some people think the roof looks like huge seashells. The roof is made of ten gigantic arched concrete shell shapes. The shells have ribs that curve inward. Concrete joins the ribs where they meet. One of the biggest cranes in the world lifted the concrete roof pieces into place. Working on the building was dangerous because of the roof.

Day #3

1. Does the Sydney Opera House look like Utson wanted it to? ___no, not exactly___
2. What clues helped you answer #1? ___Some people think it looks like seashells.___
3. How does the author describe the shape? **sails** or **shells**? ___shells___
4. What do you think the danger was with the roof? ___that the concrete pieces would fall___

The Opera House contains one hall for operas. The symphony orchestra plays concerts in another hall. A third hall is for plays. A fourth is for chamber music. The fifth is for exhibitions.

Day #4

1. What fraction of halls are used for music? ___3/5___
2. What kinds of music do symphony orchestras and chamber music groups play?   a. hip-hop   (b. classical)   c. contemporary country
3. Which, if any, of the activities that take place in the Sydney Opera House would you enjoy? ___Answers will vary.___
4. What kind of music or other event do you think they should have at the opera house? ___Answers will vary.___

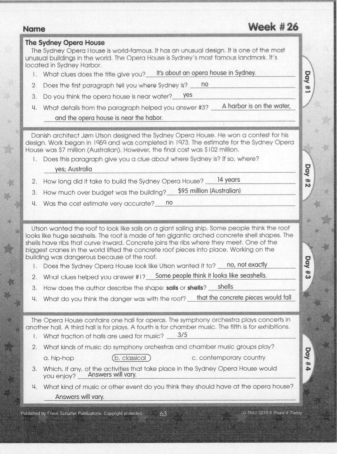

---

1. Have you ever seen a lighthouse before? ___Answers will vary.___

Assessment

Lighthouses

Imagine you're trying to get home. A storm has been raging for hours. The sea has been tossing your small sailing craft up and down, and you're not sure where you are. Suddenly in the distance, you see a faint light. You know you're safe and almost home.

2. What kind of writing does paragraph one seem like: **fiction** or **nonfiction**? ___fiction___

Lighthouses were built to guide ships into coastal waters. They were built at dangerous points on a coastline, usually near reefs or at entrances to harbors. The earliest known lighthouse was built in Egypt. It was called Pharos. Pharos was completed about 280 B.C.

3. What is the cause that leads to a lighthouse being built? ___Ships need to be guided through dangerous waters and storms.___

Boston Light was built in 1716. It was the first lighthouse in the New World. Within years, lighthouses were built in Canada and in South Carolina. By the time the Declaration of Independence was signed in 1776, there were 12 lighthouses, most in New England. In 1800, the U.S. had 16, and by 1812, there were about 49 lighthouses. The first West Coast lighthouses were completed in 1854 and 1855 in California.

4. How many years passed between the first lighthouse and the first lighthouse in the New World? (Remember that the first one was in B.C., not A.D.) ___1,996 years___

5. About how many times more lighthouses were there in 1812 than there were in 1776? ___four times___

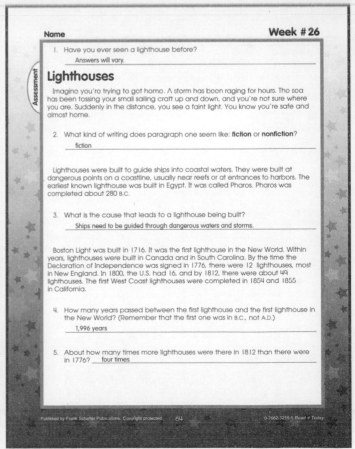

Answer Key

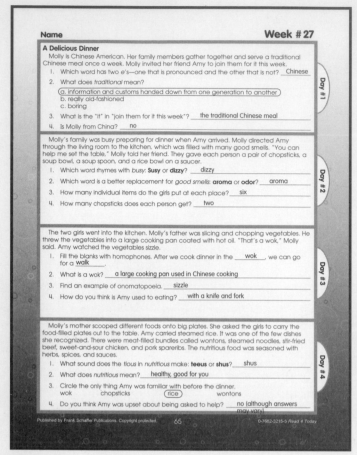

A Delicious Dinner

Molly is Chinese American. Her family members gather together and serve a traditional Chinese meal once a week. Molly invited her friend Amy to join them for it this week.

Day #1

1. Which word has two e's—one that is pronounced and the other that is not? __Chinese__
2. What does *traditional* mean?
   a. information and customs handed down from one generation to another ⟵(circled)
   b. really old-fashioned
   c. boring
3. What is the "it" in "join them for it this week"? __the traditional Chinese meal__
4. Is Molly from China? __no__

Molly's family was busy preparing for dinner when Amy arrived. Molly directed Amy through the living room to the kitchen, which was filled with many good smells. "You can help me set the table," Molly told her friend. They gave each person a pair of chopsticks, a soup bowl, a soup spoon, and a rice bowl on a saucer.

Day #2

1. Which word rhymes with *busy*: **Susy** or **dizzy**? __dizzy__
2. Which word is a better replacement for *good smells*: **aroma** or **odor**? __aroma__
3. How many individual items do the girls put at each place? __six__
4. How many chopsticks does each person get? __two__

The two girls went into the kitchen. Molly's father was slicing and chopping vegetables. He threw the vegetables into a large cooking pan coated with hot oil. "That's a wok," Molly said. Amy watched the vegetables sizzle.

Day #3

1. Fill the blanks with homophones. After we cook dinner in the __wok__, we can go for a __walk__.
2. What is a wok? __a large cooking pan used in Chinese cooking__
3. Find an example of onomatopoeia. __sizzle__
4. How do you think is Amy used to eating? __with a knife and fork__

Molly's mother scooped different foods onto big plates. She asked the girls to carry the food-filled plates out to the table. Amy carried steamed rice. It was one of the few dishes she recognized. There were meat-filled bundles called wontons, steamed noodles, stir-fried beef, sweet-and-sour chicken, and pork spareribs. The nutritious food was seasoned with herbs, spices, and sauces.

Day #4

1. What sound does the *tious* in *nutritious* make: **teeus** or **shus**? __shus__
2. What does *nutritious* mean? __healthy, good for you__
3. Circle the only thing Amy was familiar with before the dinner.
   wok   chopsticks   (rice) ⟵(circled)   wontons
4. Do you think Amy was upset about being asked to help? __no (although answers may vary)__

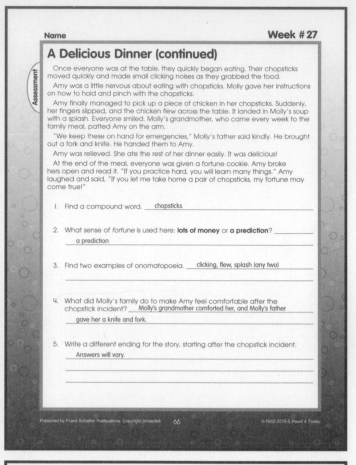

Assessment

A Delicious Dinner (continued)

Once everyone was at the table, they quickly began eating. Their chopsticks moved quickly and made small clicking noises as they grabbed the food.

Amy was a little nervous about eating with chopsticks. Molly gave her instructions on how to hold and pinch with the chopsticks.

Amy finally managed to pick up a piece of chicken in her chopsticks. Suddenly, her fingers slipped, and the chicken flew across the table. It landed in Molly's soup with a splash. Everyone smiled. Molly's grandmother, who came every week to the family meal, patted Amy on the arm.

"We keep these on hand for emergencies," Molly's father said kindly. He brought out a fork and knife. He handed them to Amy.

Amy was relieved. She ate the rest of her dinner easily. It was delicious!

At the end of the meal, everyone was given a fortune cookie. Amy broke hers open and read it. "If you practice hard, you will learn many things." Amy laughed and said, "If you let me take home a pair of chopsticks, my fortune may come true!"

1. Find a compound word. __chopsticks__
2. What sense of *fortune* is used here: **lots of money** or **a prediction**? __a prediction__
3. Find two examples of onomatopoeia. __clicking, flew, splash (any two)__
4. What did Molly's family do to make Amy feel comfortable after the chopstick incident? __Molly's grandmother comforted her, and Molly's father gave her a knife and fork.__
5. Write a different ending for the story, starting after the chopstick incident. __Answers will vary.__

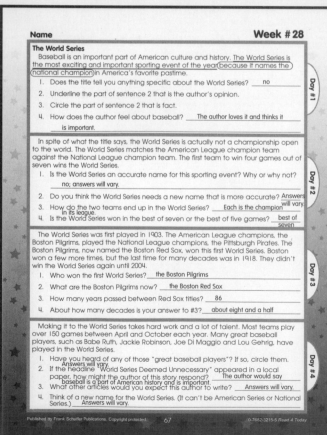

The World Series

Baseball is an important part of American culture and history. The World Series is the most exciting and important sporting event of the year (because it names the national champion) in America's favorite pastime.

Day #1

1. Does the title tell you anything specific about the World Series? __no__
2. Underline the part of sentence 2 that is the author's opinion.
3. Circle the part of sentence 2 that is fact.
4. How does the author feel about baseball? __The author loves it and thinks it is important.__

In spite of what the title says, the World Series is actually not a championship open to the world. The World Series matches the American League champion team against the National League champion team. The first team to win four games out of seven wins the World Series.

Day #2

1. Is the World Series an accurate name for this sporting event? Why or why not? __no; answers will vary.__
2. Do you think the World Series needs a new name that is more accurate? __Answers will vary.__
3. How do the two teams end up in the World Series? __Each is the champion in its league.__
4. Is the World Series won in the best of seven or the best of five games? __best of seven__

The World Series was first played in 1903. The American League champions, the Boston Pilgrims, played the National League champions, the Pittsburgh Pirates. The Boston Pilgrims, now named the Boston Red Sox, won this first World Series. Boston won a few more times, but the last time for many decades was in 1918. They didn't win the World Series again until 2004.

Day #3

1. Who won the first World Series? __the Boston Pilgrims__
2. What are the Boston Pilgrims now? __the Boston Red Sox__
3. How many years passed between Red Sox titles? __86__
4. About how many decades is your answer to #3? __about eight and a half__

Making it to the World Series takes hard work and a lot of talent. Most teams play over 150 games between April and October each year. Many great baseball players, such as Babe Ruth, Jackie Robinson, Joe Di Maggio and Lou Gehrig, have played in the World Series.

Day #4

1. Have you heard of any of those "great baseball players"? If so, circle them. __Answers will vary.__
2. If the headline "World Series Deemed Unnecessary" appeared in a local paper, how might the author of this story respond? __The author would say baseball is a part of American history and is important.__
3. What other articles would you expect this author to write? __Answers will vary.__
4. Think of a new name for the World Series. (It can't be American Series or National Series.) __Answers will vary.__

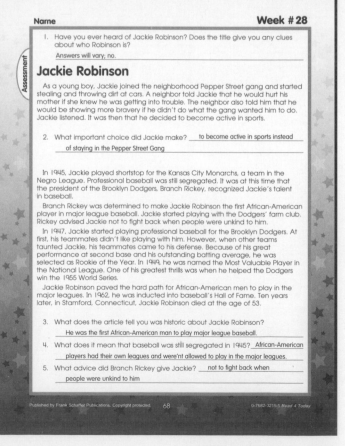

1. Have you ever heard of Jackie Robinson? Does the title give you any clues about who Robinson is? __Answers will vary; no.__

Assessment

Jackie Robinson

As a young boy, Jackie joined the neighborhood Pepper Street gang and started stealing and throwing dirt at cars. A neighbor told Jackie that he would hurt his mother if she knew he was getting into trouble. The neighbor also told him that he would be showing more bravery if he didn't do what the gang wanted him to do. Jackie listened. It was then that he decided to become active in sports.

2. What important choice did Jackie make? __to become active in sports instead of staying in the Pepper Street Gang__

In 1945, Jackie played shortstop for the Kansas City Monarchs, a team in the Negro League. Professional baseball was still segregated. It was at this time that the president of the Brooklyn Dodgers, Branch Rickey, recognized Jackie's talent in baseball.

Branch Rickey was determined to make Jackie Robinson the first African-American player in major league baseball. Jackie started playing with the Dodgers' farm club. Rickey advised Jackie not to fight back when people were unkind to him.

In 1947, Jackie started playing professional baseball for the Brooklyn Dodgers. At first, his teammates didn't like playing with him. However, when other teams taunted Jackie, his teammates came to his defense. Because of his great performance at second base and his outstanding batting average, he was selected as Rookie of the Year. In 1949, he was named the Most Valuable Player in the National League. One of his greatest thrills was when he helped the Dodgers win the 1955 World Series.

Jackie Robinson paved the hard path for African-American men to play in the major leagues. In 1962, he was inducted into baseball's Hall of Fame. Ten years later, in Stamford, Connecticut, Jackie Robinson died at the age of 53.

3. What does the article tell you was historic about Jackie Robinson? __He was the first African-American man to play major league baseball.__
4. What does it mean that baseball was still segregated in 1945? __African-American players had their own leagues and were'nt allowed to play in the major leagues.__
5. What advice did Branch Rickey give Jackie? __not to fight back when people were unkind to him__

Answer Key

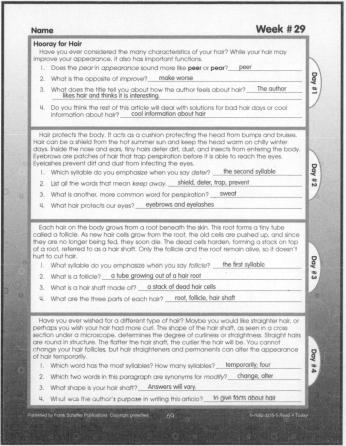

Hooray for Hair

Have you ever considered the many characteristics of your hair? While your hair may improve your appearance, it also has important functions.

Day #1

1. Does the *pear* in *appearance* sound more like **peer** or **pear**? ___peer___

2. What is the opposite of *improve*? ___make worse___

3. What does the title tell you about how the author feels about hair? ___The author likes hair and thinks it is interesting.___

4. Do you think the rest of the article will deal with solutions for bad hair days or cool information about hair? ___cool information about hair___

Hair protects the body. It acts as a cushion protecting the head from bumps and bruises. Hair can be a shield from the hot summer sun and keep the head warm on chilly winter days. Inside the nose and ears, tiny hairs deter dirt, dust, and insects from entering the body. Eyebrows are patches of hair that trap perspiration before it is able to reach the eyes. Eyelashes prevent dirt and dust from infecting the eyes.

Day #2

1. Which syllable do you emphasize when you say *deter*? ___the second syllable___

2. List all the words that mean *keep away*. ___shield, deter, trap, prevent___

3. What is another, more common word for perspiration? ___sweat___

4. What hair protects our eyes? ___eyebrows and eyelashes___

Each hair on the body grows from a root beneath the skin. This root forms a tiny tube called a follicle. As new hair cells grow from the root, the old cells are pushed up, and since they are no longer being fed, they soon die. The dead cells harden, forming a stack on top of a root, referred to as a hair shaft. Only the follicle and the root remain alive, so it doesn't hurt to cut hair.

Day #3

1. What syllable do you emphasize when you say *follicle*? ___the first syllable___

2. What is a follicle? ___a tube growing out of a hair root___

3. What is a hair shaft made of? ___a stack of dead hair cells___

4. What are the three parts of each hair? ___root, follicle, hair shaft___

Have you ever wished for a different type of hair? Maybe you would like straighter hair, or perhaps you wish your hair had more curl. The shape of the hair shaft, as seen in a cross section under a microscope, determines the degree of curliness or straightness. Straight hairs are round in structure. The flatter the hair shaft, the curlier the hair will be. You cannot change your hair follicles, but hair straighteners and permanents can alter the appearance of hair temporarily.

Day #4

1. Which word has the most syllables? How many syllables? ___temporarily; four___

2. Which two words in this paragraph are synonyms for *modify*? ___change, alter___

3. What shape is your hair shaft? ___Answers will vary.___

4. What was the author's purpose in writing this article? ___to give facts about hair___

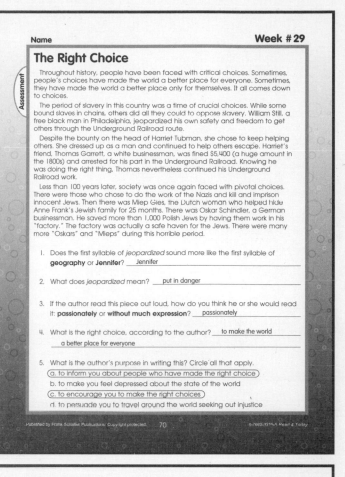

The Right Choice

Assessment

Throughout history, people have been faced with critical choices. Sometimes, people's choices have made the world a better place for everyone. Sometimes, they have made the world a better place only for themselves. It all comes down to choices.

The period of slavery in this country was a time of crucial choices. While some bound slaves in chains, others did all they could to oppose slavery. William Still, a free black man in Philadelphia, jeopardized his own safety and freedom to get others through the Underground Railroad route.

Despite the bounty on the head of Harriet Tubman, she chose to keep helping others. She dressed up as a man and continued to help others escape. Harriet's friend, Thomas Garrett, a white businessman, was fined $5,400 (a huge amount in the 1800s) and arrested for his part in the Underground Railroad. Knowing he was doing the right thing, Thomas nevertheless continued his Underground Railroad work.

Less than 100 years later, society was once again faced with pivotal choices. There were those who chose to do the work of the Nazis and kill and imprison innocent Jews. Then there was Miep Gies, the Dutch woman who helped hide Anne Frank's Jewish family for 25 months. There was Oskar Schindler, a German businessman. He saved more than 1,000 Polish Jews by having them work in his "factory." The factory was actually a safe haven for the Jews. There were many more "Oskars" and "Mieps" during this horrible period.

1. Does the first syllable of *jeopardized* sound more like the first syllable of **geography** or **Jennifer**? ___Jennifer___

2. What does *jeopardized* mean? ___put in danger___

3. If the author read this piece out loud, how do you think he or she would read it: **passionately** or **without much expression**? ___passionately___

4. What is the right choice, according to the author? ___to make the world a better place for everyone___

5. What is the author's purpose in writing this? Circle all that apply.
   (a. to inform you about people who have made the right choice)
   b. to make you feel depressed about the state of the world
   (c. to encourage you to make the right choices)
   d. to persuade you to travel around the world seeking out injustice

---

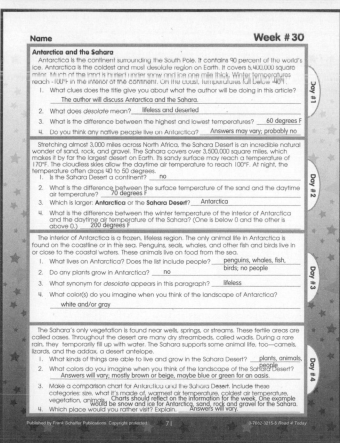

Antarctica and the Sahara

Antarctica is the continent surrounding the South Pole. It contains 90 percent of the world's ice. Antarctica is the coldest and most desolate region on Earth. It covers 5,400,000 square miles. Much of the land is buried under snow and ice one mile thick. Winter temperatures reach -100°F in the interior of the continent. On the coast, temperatures fall below -40°F.

Day #1

1. What clues does the title give you about what the author will be doing in this article? ___The author will discuss Antarctica and the Sahara.___

2. What does *desolate* mean? ___lifeless and deserted___

3. What is the difference between the highest and lowest temperatures? ___60 degrees F___

4. Do you think any native people live on Antarctica? ___Answers may vary; probably no___

Stretching almost 3,000 miles across North Africa, the Sahara Desert is an incredible natural wonder of sand, rock, and gravel. The Sahara covers over 3,500,000 square miles, which makes it by far the largest desert on Earth. Its sandy surface may reach a temperature of 170°F. The cloudless skies allow the daytime air temperature to reach 100°F. At night, the temperature often drops 40 to 50 degrees.

Day #2

1. Is the Sahara Desert a continent? ___no___

2. What is the difference between the surface temperature of the sand and the daytime air temperature? ___70 degrees F___

3. Which is larger: **Antarctica** or the **Sahara Desert**? ___Antarctica___

4. What is the difference between the winter temperature of the interior of Antarctica and the daytime air temperature of the Sahara? (One is below 0 and the other is above 0.) ___200 degrees F___

The interior of Antarctica is a frozen, lifeless region. The only animal life in Antarctica is found on the coastline or in the sea. Penguins, seals, whales, and other fish and birds live in or close to the coastal waters. These animals live on food from the sea.

Day #3

1. What lives on Antarctica? Does the list include people? ___penguins, whales, fish, birds; no people___

2. Do any plants grow in Antarctica? ___no___

3. What synonym for *desolate* appears in this paragraph? ___lifeless___

4. What color(s) do you imagine when you think of the landscape of Antarctica? ___white and/or gray___

The Sahara's only vegetation is found near wells, springs, or streams. These fertile areas are called oases. Throughout the desert are many dry streambeds, called wadis. During a rare rain, they temporarily fill up with water. The Sahara supports some animal life, too—camels, lizards, and the addax, a desert antelope.

Day #4

1. What kinds of things are able to live and grow in the Sahara Desert? ___plants, animals, people___

2. What colors do you imagine when you think of the landscape of the Sahara Desert? ___Answers will vary; mostly brown or beige, maybe blue or green for an oasis___

3. Make a comparison chart for Antarctica and the Sahara Desert. Include these categories: size, what it's made of, warmest air temperature, coldest air temperature, vegetation, animals. ___Charts should reflect on the information for the week. One example would be snow and ice for Antarctica, sand, rock and gravel for the Sahara.___

4. Which place would you rather visit? Explain. ___Answers will vary.___

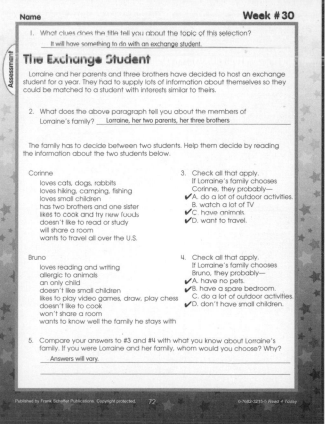

1. What clues does the title tell you about the topic of this selection? ___It will have something to do with an exchange student.___

The Exchange Student

Assessment

Lorraine and her parents and three brothers have decided to host an exchange student for a year. They had to supply lots of information about themselves so they could be matched to a student with interests similar to theirs.

2. What does the above paragraph tell you about the members of Lorraine's family? ___Lorraine, her two parents, her three brothers___

The family has to decide between two students. Help them decide by reading the information about the two students below.

Corinne
loves cats, dogs, rabbits
loves hiking, camping, fishing
loves small children
has two brothers and one sister
likes to cook and try new foods
doesn't like to read or study
will share a room
wants to travel all over the U.S.

3. Check all that apply.
If Lorraine's family chooses Corinne, they probably—
✔ A. do a lot of outdoor activities.
 B. watch a lot of TV
✔ C. have animals.
✔ D. want to travel.

Bruno
loves reading and writing
allergic to animals
an only child
doesn't like small children
likes to play video games, draw, play chess
doesn't like to cook
won't share a room
wants to know well the family he stays with

4. Check all that apply.
If Lorraine's family chooses Bruno, they probably—
✔ A. have no pets.
✔ B. have a spare bedroom.
 C. do a lot of outdoor activities.
✔ D. don't have small children.

5. Compare your answers to #3 and #4 with what you know about Lorraine's family. If you were Lorraine and her family, whom would you choose? Why? ___Answers will vary.___

Answer Key

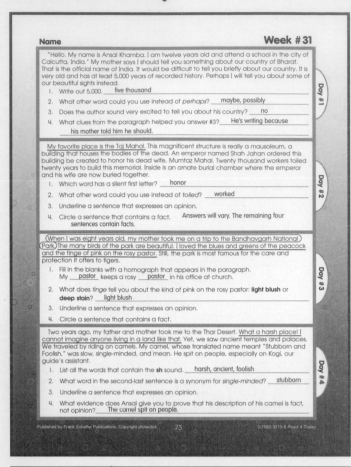

"Hello. My name is Ansal Khamba. I am twelve years old and attend a school in the city of Calcutta, India." My mother says I should tell you something about our country of Bharat. That is the official name of India. It would be difficult to tell you briefly about our country. It is very old and has at least 5,000 years of recorded history. Perhaps I will tell you about some of our beautiful sights instead.

1. Write out 5,000. ___five thousand___
2. What other word could you use instead of *perhaps*? ___maybe, possibly___
3. Does the author sound very excited to tell you about his country? ___no___
4. What clues from the paragraph helped you answer #3? ___He's writing because his mother told him he should.___

Day #1

My favorite place is the Taj Mahal. This magnificent structure is really a mausoleum, a building that houses the bodies of the dead. An emperor named Shah Jahan ordered this building to be created to honor his dead wife, Mumtaz Mahal. Twenty thousand workers toiled twenty years to build this memorial. Inside is an ornate burial chamber where the emperor and his wife are now buried together.

1. Which word has a silent first letter? ___honor___
2. What other word could you use instead of *toiled*? ___worked___
3. Underline a sentence that expresses an opinion.
4. Circle a sentence that contains a fact. ___Answers will vary. The remaining four sentences contain facts.___

Day #2

(When I was eight years old, my mother took me on a trip to the Bandhavgarh National Park.) The many birds of the park are beautiful. I loved the blues and greens of the peacock and the tinge of pink on the rosy pastor. Still, the park is most famous for the care and protection it offers to tigers.

1. Fill in the blanks with a homograph that appears in the paragraph. My ___pastor___ keeps a rosy ___pastor___ in his office at church.
2. What does *tinge* tell you about the kind of pink on the rosy pastor: **light blush** or **deep stain**? ___light blush___
3. Underline a sentence that expresses an opinion.
4. Circle a sentence that contains a fact.

Day #3

Two years ago, my father and mother took me to the Thar Desert. What a harsh place! I cannot imagine anyone living in a land like that. Yet, we saw ancient temples and palaces. We traveled by riding on camels. My camel, whose translated name meant "Stubborn and Foolish," was slow, single-minded, and mean. He spit on people, especially on Kogi, our guide's assistant.

1. List all the words that contain the **sh** sound. ___harsh, ancient, foolish___
2. What word in the second-last sentence is a synonym for *single-minded*? ___stubborn___
3. Underline a sentence that expresses an opinion.
4. What evidence does Ansal give you to prove that his description of his camel is fact, not opinion? ___The camel spit on people.___

Day #4

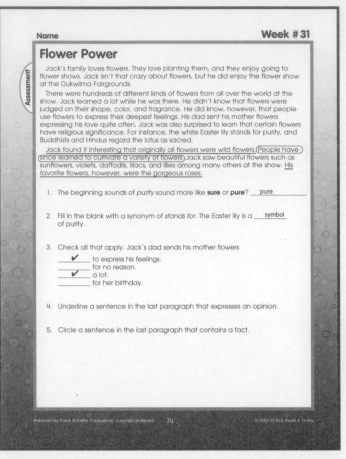

Flower Power

Assessment

Jack's family loves flowers. They love planting them, and they enjoy going to flower shows. Jack isn't that crazy about flowers, but he did enjoy the flower show at the Dukwilma Fairgrounds.

There were hundreds of different kinds of flowers from all over the world at the show. Jack learned a lot while he was there. He didn't know that flowers were judged on their shape, color, and fragrance. He did know, however, that people use flowers to express their deepest feelings. His dad sent his mother flowers expressing his love quite often. Jack was also surprised to learn that certain flowers have religious significance. For instance, the white Easter lily stands for purity, and Buddhists and Hindus regard the lotus as sacred.

Jack found it interesting that originally all flowers were wild flowers. (People have since learned to cultivate a variety of flowers.) Jack saw beautiful flowers such as sunflowers, violets, daffodils, lilacs, and lilies among many others at the show. His favorite flowers, however, were the gorgeous roses.

1. The beginning sounds of *purity* sound more like **sure** or **pure**? ___pure___
2. Fill in the blank with a synonym of *stands for*. The Easter lily is a ___symbol___ of purity.
3. Check all that apply. Jack's dad sends his mother flowers
   - ___✔___ to express his feelings.
   - _____ for no reason.
   - ___✔___ a lot.
   - _____ for her birthday.
4. Underline a sentence in the last paragraph that expresses an opinion.
5. Circle a sentence in the last paragraph that contains a fact.

Lazy Time
Sally and Ned are swaying slowly in the family swing.

1. What does the title tell us about the story? ___It will be about a lazy time.___
2. What information does the opening sentence add? ___Sally and Ned are in a swing.___
3. Is there an image in the first sentence that supports or illustrates the title? ___yes___
4. If so, what is it and how does it illustrate the title? ___They are swaying slowly. If it weren't a lazy time, they wouldn't be in a swing or they would be swinging quickly.___

Day #1

The air is crisp. Sally puts her arm around Ned and snuggles into his shaggy body. Ned's tongue licks Sally's hand that lies on her blue-jeaned leg. They watch a sluggish ladybug crawl underneath a pile of old, brown leaves. One red leaf drifts down to the top of the ladybug's leaf pile.

1. What time of year is it? ___fall___
2. What clues helped you answer #1? ___The air is crisp, and leaves are falling.___
3. What or who do you think Ned is? ___a dog___
4. What clues helped you answer #3? ___His body is shaggy. He licks Sally's hand.___

Day #2

Ned's graying ears prick up as a southbound V of geese honks goodbye. The sky slowly turns from blue, to pink, to purple, to black.
The first star shines as Sally's mom calls her in to eat. Sally gives a last push as she slides out of the swing. She walks to the back door of the house. Ned leaps down.

1. What sounds can you hear in this selection? ___geese honking, mom calling___
2. Is Ned a puppy or an older dog? ___an older dog___
3. What clues helped you answer #2? ___His ears are graying.___
4. How do you think Sally feels? ___Answers may vary; probably happy___

Day #3

Ned barks once at a rabbit, and then chases after Sally. She smiles and rubs Ned's head as they walk into the warm house together.

1. What meal is Sally about to eat? ___dinner___
2. Did the title set up the story well? ___yes___
3. List the words in all the selections that give a picture of laziness. ___swaying, slowly, sluggish, drifts, slowly turns, walks___
4. What other title would work? ___Answers will vary.___

Day #4

---

1. This is a table of contents for a book. What does a table of contents tell you? ___the names of chapters in the book and what pages they're on___

A Year in My Life

Assessment

CONTENTS

2. What time of year is it in chapters 2 and 3? ___fall___

3. What season is it in chapters 7–9? ___spring___

4. Do you think chapter 13 is about the harvest festival of Thanksgiving or about the author harvesting food from a garden? What clues helped you answer that question? ___harvesting food from a garden, because there's already a chapter about Thanksgiving (3), and in chapter 11 the author tends a garden___
5. Is the book arranged thematically (by theme) or chronologically (by time)? ___chronologically___

Answer Key

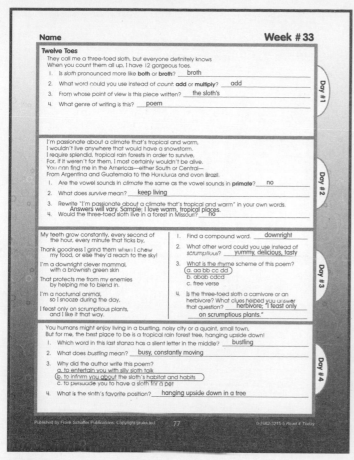

Week # 33

Name

Twelve Toes
They call me a three-toed sloth, but everyone definitely knows
When you count them all up, I have 12 gorgeous toes.

Day #1
1. Is *sloth* pronounced more like **both** or **broth**? __broth__
2. What word could you use instead of *count*: **add** or **multiply**? __add__
3. From whose point of view is this piece written? __the sloth's__
4. What genre of writing is this? __poem__

I'm passionate about a climate that's tropical and warm,
I wouldn't live anywhere that would have a snowstorm.
I require splendid, tropical rain forests in order to survive.
For, if it weren't for them, I most certainly wouldn't be alive.
You can find me in the Americas—either South or Central—
From Argentina and Guatemala to the Honduras and even Brazil.

Day #2
1. Are the vowel sounds in *climate* the same as the vowel sounds in **primate**? __no__
2. What does *survive* mean? __keep living__
3. Rewrite "I'm passionate about a climate that's tropical and warm" in your own words.
   Answers will vary. Sample: I love warm, tropical places.
4. Would the three-toed sloth live in a forest in Missouri? __no__

My teeth grow constantly, every second of
the hour, every minute that ticks by.

Thank goodness I grind them when I chew
my food, or else they'd reach to the sky!

I'm a downright clever mammal,
with a brownish green skin

That protects me from my enemies
by helping me to blend in.

I'm a nocturnal animal,
so I snooze during the day.

I feast only on scrumptious plants,
and I like it that way.

Day #3
1. Find a compound word. __downright__
2. What other word could you use instead of *scrumptious*? __yummy, delicious, tasty__
3. What is the rhyme scheme of this poem?
   (a. aa bb cc dd)
   b. abab cdcd
   c. free verse
4. Is the three-toed sloth a carnivore or an herbivore? What clues helped you answer that question? __herbivore; "I feast only on scrumptious plants."__

You humans might enjoy living in a bustling, noisy city or a quaint, small town,
But for me, the best place to be is a tropical rain forest tree, hanging upside down!

Day #4
1. Which word in this last stanza has a silent letter in the middle? __bustling__
2. What does *bustling* mean? __busy, constantly moving__
3. Why did the author write this poem?
   a. to entertain you with silly sloth talk
   (b. to inform you about the sloth's habitat and habits)
   c. to persuade you to have a sloth for a pet
4. What is the sloth's favorite position? __hanging upside down in a tree__

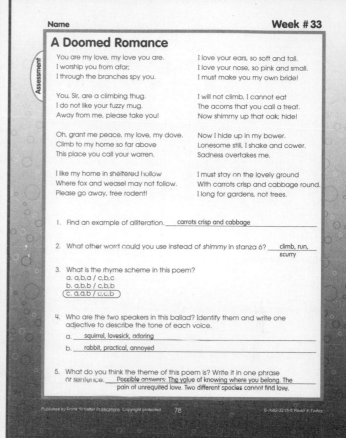

Week # 33

Name

Assessment

A Doomed Romance

You are my love, my love you are.
I worship you from afar;
I through the branches spy you.

You, Sir, are a climbing thug.
I do not like your fuzzy mug.
Away from me, please take you!

Oh, grant me peace, my love, my dove.
Climb to my home so far above
This place you call your warren.

I like my home in sheltered hollow
Where fox and weasel may not follow.
Please go away, tree rodent!

I love your ears, so soft and tall.
I love your nose, so pink and small.
I must make you my own bride!

I will not climb, I cannot eat
The acorns that you call a treat.
Now shimmy up that oak; hide!

Now I hide up in my bower.
Lonesome still, I shake and cower.
Sadness overtakes me.

I must stay on the lovely ground
With carrots crisp and cabbage round.
I long for gardens, not trees.

1. Find an example of alliteration. __carrots crisp and cabbage__

2. What other word could you use instead of *shimmy* in stanza 6? __climb, run, scurry__

3. What is the rhyme scheme in this poem?
   a. a,b,a / c,b,c
   b. a,b,b / c,b,b
   (c. a,a,b / c,c,b)

4. Who are the two speakers in this ballad? Identify them and write one adjective to describe the tone of each voice.
   a. __squirrel, lovesick, adoring__
   b. __rabbit, practical, annoyed__

5. What do you think the theme of this poem is? Write it in one phrase or sentence. __Possible answers: The value of knowing where you belong. The pain of unrequited love. Two different species cannot find love.__

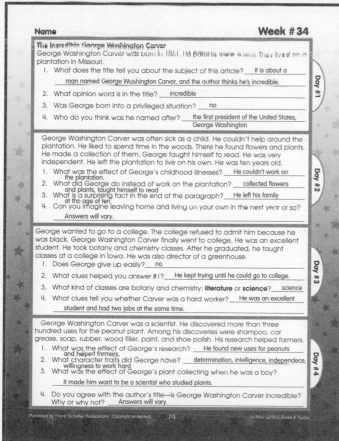

Week # 34

Name

The Incredible George Washington Carver
George Washington Carver was born in 1861. His parents were slaves. They lived on a plantation in Missouri.

Day #1
1. What does the title tell you about the subject of this article? __It is about a man named George Washington Carver, and the author thinks he's incredible.__
2. What opinion word is in the title? __incredible__
3. Was George born into a privileged situation? __no__
4. Who do you think was he named after? __the first president of the United States, George Washington__

George Washington Carver was often sick as a child. He couldn't help around the plantation. He liked to spend time in the woods. There he found flowers and plants. He made a collection of them. George taught himself to read. He was very independent. He left the plantation to live on his own. He was ten years old.

Day #2
1. What was the effect of George's childhood illnesses? __He couldn't work on the plantation.__
2. What did George do instead of work on the plantation? __collected flowers and plants, taught himself to read__
3. What is a surprising fact in the end of the paragraph? __He left his family at the age of ten.__
4. Can you imagine leaving home and living on your own in the next year or so? __Answers will vary.__

George wanted to go to a college. The college refused to admit him because he was black. George Washington Carver finally went to college. He was an excellent student. He took botany and chemistry classes. After he graduated, he taught classes at a college in Iowa. He was also director of a greenhouse.

Day #3
1. Does George give up easily? __no__
2. What clues helped you answer #1? __He kept trying until he could go to college.__
3. What kind of classes are botany and chemistry: **literature** or **science**? __science__
4. What clues tell you whether Carver was a hard worker? __He was an excellent student and had two jobs at the same time.__

George Washington Carver was a scientist. He discovered more than three hundred uses for the peanut plant. Among his discoveries were shampoo, car grease, soap, rubber, wood filler, paint, and shoe polish. His research helped farmers.

Day #4
1. What was the effect of George's research? __He found new uses for peanuts and helped farmers.__
2. What character traits did George have? __determination, intelligence, independence, willingness to work hard__
3. What was the effect of George's plant collecting when he was a boy? __It made him want to be a scientist who studied plants.__
4. Do you agree with the author's title—is George Washington Carver incredible? Why or why not? __Answers will vary.__

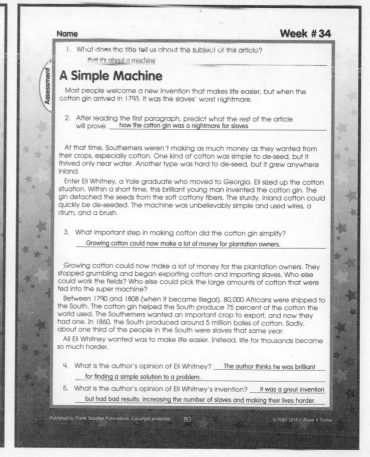

Week # 34

Name

1. What does the title tell us about the subject of this article? __that it's about a machine__

Assessment

A Simple Machine
Most people welcome a new invention that makes life easier, but when the cotton gin arrived in 1793, it was the slaves' worst nightmare.

2. After reading the first paragraph, predict what the rest of the article will prove. __how the cotton gin was a nightmare for slaves__

At that time, Southerners weren't making as much money as they wanted from their crops, especially cotton. One kind of cotton was simple to de-seed, but it thrived only near water. Another type was hard to de-seed, but it grew anywhere inland.

Enter Eli Whitney, a Yale graduate who moved to Georgia. Eli sized up the cotton situation. Within a short time, this brilliant young man invented the cotton gin. The gin detached the seeds from the soft cottony fibers. The sturdy, inland cotton could quickly be de-seeded. The machine was unbelievably simple and used wires, a drum, and a brush.

3. What important step in making cotton did the cotton gin simplify? __Growing cotton could now make a lot of money for plantation owners.__

Growing cotton could now make a lot of money for the plantation owners. They stopped grumbling and began exporting cotton and importing slaves. Who else could work the fields? Who else could pick the large amounts of cotton that were fed into the master's machine?

Between 1790 and 1808 (when it became illegal), 80,000 Africans were shipped to the South. The cotton gin helped the South produce 75 percent of the cotton the world used. The Southerners wanted an important crop to export, and now they had one. In 1860, the South produced around 5 million bales of cotton. Sadly, about one third of the people in the South were slaves that same year.

All Eli Whitney wanted was to make life easier. Instead, life for thousands became so much harder.

4. What is the author's opinion of Eli Whitney? __The author thinks he was brilliant for finding a simple solution to a problem.__
5. What is the author's opinion of Eli Whitney's invention? __It was a great invention but had bad results: increasing the number of slaves and making their lives harder.__

Answer Key

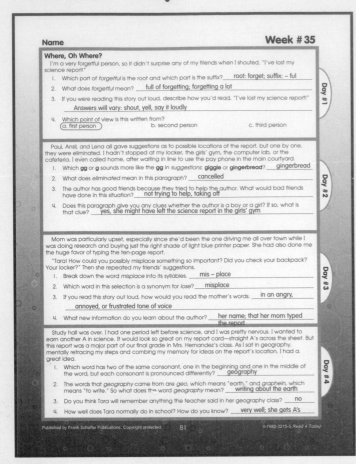

Name

Week # 35

Where, Oh Where?

I'm a very forgetful person, so it didn't surprise any of my friends when I shouted, "I've lost my science report!"

Day #1

1. Which part of *forgetful* is the root and which part is the suffix? ___root: forget; suffix – ful___

2. What does *forgetful* mean? ___full of forgetting; forgetting a lot___

3. If you were reading this story out loud, describe how you'd read, "I've lost my science report!" ___Answers will vary: shout, yell, say it loudly___

4. Which point of view is this written from?
   (a. first person)   b. second person   c. third person

Day #2

Paul, Ansil, and Lena all gave suggestions as to possible locations of the report, but one by one, they were eliminated. I hadn't stopped at my locker, the girls' gym, the computer lab, or the cafeteria. I even called home, after waiting in line to use the pay phone in the main courtyard.

1. Which **gg** or **g** sounds more like the **gg** in *suggestions*: **giggle** or **gingerbread**? ___gingerbread___

2. What does *eliminated* mean in this paragraph? ___cancelled___

3. The author has good friends because they tried to help the author. What would bad friends have done in this situation? ___not trying to help, taking off___

4. Does this paragraph give you any clues whether the author is a boy or a girl? If so, what is that clue? ___yes, she might have left the science report in the girls' gym___

Day #3

Mom was particularly upset, especially since she'd been the one driving me all over town while I was doing research and buying just the right shade of light blue printer paper. She had also done me the huge favor of typing the ten-page report.

"Tara! How could you possibly misplace something so important? Did you check your backpack? Your locker?" Then she repeated my friends' suggestions.

1. Break down the word *misplace* into its syllables. ___mis – place___

2. Which word in this selection is a synonym for *lose*? ___misplace___

3. If you read this story out loud, how would you read the mother's words? ___in an angry, annoyed, or frustrated tone of voice___

4. What new information do you learn about the author? ___her name; that her mom typed the report___

Day #4

Study hall was over. I had one period left before science, and I was pretty nervous. I wanted to earn another A in science. It would look so great on my report card—straight A's across the sheet. But this report was a major part of our final grade in Mrs. Hernandez's class. As I sat in geography, mentally retracing my steps and combing my memory for ideas on the report's location, I had a great idea.

1. Which word has two of the same consonant, one in the beginning and one in the middle of the word, but each consonant is pronounced differently? ___geography___

2. The words that *geography* came from are *geo*, which means "earth," and *graphein*, which means "to write." So what does the word *geography* mean? ___writing about the earth___

3. Do you think Tara will remember anything the teacher said in her geography class? ___no___

4. How well does Tara normally do in school? How do you know? ___very well; she gets A's___

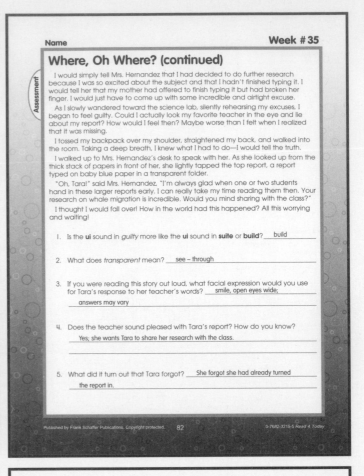

Name

Week # 35

Assessment

Where, Oh Where? (continued)

I would simply tell Mrs. Hernandez that I had decided to do further research because I was so excited about the subject and that I hadn't finished typing it. I would tell her that my mother had offered to finish typing it but had broken her finger. I would just have to come up with some incredible and airtight excuse.

As I slowly wandered toward the science lab, silently rehearsing my excuses, I began to feel guilty. Could I actually look my favorite teacher in the eye and lie about my report? How would I feel then? Maybe worse than I felt when I realized that it was missing.

I tossed my backpack over my shoulder, straightened my back, and walked into the room. Taking a deep breath, I knew what I had to do—I would tell the truth.

I walked up to Mrs. Hernandez's desk to speak with her. As she looked up from the thick stack of papers in front of her, she lightly tapped the top report, a report typed on baby blue paper in a transparent folder.

"Oh, Tara!" said Mrs. Hernandez, "I'm always glad when one or two students hand in these larger reports early. I can really take my time reading them then. Your research on whale migration is incredible. Would you mind sharing with the class?"

I thought I would fall over! How in the world had this happened? All this worrying and waiting!

1. Is the **ui** sound in *guilty* more like the **ui** sound in **suite** or **build**? ___build___

2. What does *transparent* mean? ___see – through___

3. If you were reading this story out loud, what facial expression would you use for Tara's response to her teacher's words? ___smile, open eyes wide; answers may vary___

4. Does the teacher sound pleased with Tara's report? How do you know? ___Yes; she wants Tara to share her research with the class.___

5. What did it turn out that Tara forgot? ___She forgot she had already turned the report in.___

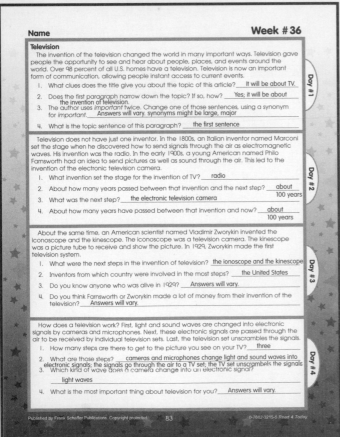

Name

Week # 36

Television

The invention of the television changed the world in many important ways. Television gave people the opportunity to see and hear about people, places, and events around the world. Over 98 percent of all U.S. homes have a television. Television is now an important form of communication, allowing people instant access to current events.

Day #1

1. What clues does the title give you about the topic of this article? ___It will be about TV.___

2. Does the first paragraph narrow down the topic? If so, how? ___Yes; it will be about the invention of television.___

3. The author uses *important* twice. Change one of those sentences, using a synonym for *important*. ___Answers will vary. synonyms might be large, major___

4. What is the topic sentence of this paragraph? ___the first sentence___

Day #2

Television does not have just one inventor. In the 1800s, an Italian inventor named Marconi set the stage when he discovered how to send signals through the air as electromagnetic waves. His invention was the radio. In the early 1900s, a young American named Philo Farnsworth had an idea to send pictures as well as sound through the air. This led to the invention of the electronic television camera.

1. What invention set the stage for the invention of TV? ___radio___

2. About how many years passed between that invention and the next step? ___about 100 years___

3. What was the next step? ___the electronic television camera___

4. About how many years have passed between that invention and now? ___about 100 years___

Day #3

About the same time, an American scientist named Vladimir Zworykin invented the iconoscope and the kinescope. The iconoscope was a television camera. The kinescope was a picture tube to receive and show the picture. In 1929, Zworykin made the first television system.

1. What were the next steps in the invention of television? ___the ionoscope and the kinescope___

2. Inventors from which country were involved in the most steps? ___the United States___

3. Do you know anyone who was alive in 1929? ___Answers will vary.___

4. Do you think Farnsworth or Zworykin made a lot of money from their invention of the television? ___Answers will vary.___

Day #4

How does a television work? First, light and sound waves are changed into electronic signals by cameras and microphones. Next, these electronic signals are passed through the air to be received by individual television sets. Last, the television set unscrambles the signals.

1. How many steps are there to get to the picture you see on your TV? ___three___

2. What are those steps? ___cameras and microphones change light and sound waves into electronic signals; the signals go through the air to a TV set; the TV set unscrambles the signals___

3. Which kind of wave does a camera change into an electronic signal? ___light waves___

4. What is the most important thing about television for you? ___Answers will vary.___

Name

Week # 36

1. Have you ever heard of Philo Farnsworth? ___yes (This answer supposes that student read the previous excerpts.)___

Assessment

Philo Farnsworth and Television

What would you say if someone asked who had invented the transmission, or sending, of television images? If you do not know the answer, you are not alone. Most people do not know that this was an invention of Philo Farnsworth. This is probably because a large company took Farnsworth's idea.

2. Why have most people not heard of Philo Farnsworth? ___because a large company took his idea___

Farnsworth was born in a log cabin in 1906. When he was twelve, his family moved to a ranch. This put Farnsworth miles away from his school, and he rode his horse to get there.

Farnsworth was very interested in the electron and electricity. He asked one of his teachers to teach him outside of class and to let him sit in on a course for older students. The teacher agreed. He came up with the idea for sending television pictures when he was only fourteen.

3. What year did Farnsworth have the idea? ___1920___

An article told of his invention when he was only twenty-two. How did it work? Moving images, or pictures, were broken into pinpoints of light. These pinpoints were changed into electrical impulses, or movements. Then the impulses were collected by the television set and changed back to light. People could see the images. A major magazine listed Farnsworth as one of the 100 greatest scientists and thinkers of the twentieth century.

4. What year did the article appear in? ___1928___

5. Do you think Farnsworth made a lot of money from his invention of television? Explain your reasoning. ___Answers will vary.___

Answer Key

Baby, It's Cold Outside!

Picture yourself as a geologist studying Earth's outer shell. You are at the end of Earth, occupying a research station on the coldest continent in the world. You are at a place where no people live permanently. You are on the continent of Antarctica.

Day #1

1. List all the words with four syllables. __geologist, permanently, Antarctica__
2. What does it mean to live somewhere permanently? __to live there all the time__
3. What is the purpose of the first paragraph? __to encourage you to think of yourself as a researcher in Antarctica__
4. Which continent is the coldest? __Antarctica__

You are not alone. There are about 40 permanent research stations on this icy mass. Scientists, medical researchers, and biologists are all here. They come from about thirty countries to learn more about this frigid area.

Day #2

1. Is the **g** in *frigid* a hard **g** or a soft **g**? __soft g__
2. List all the words in this paragraph that have to do with how cold Antarctica is. __icy, frigid__
3. What is the main idea of this paragraph? __Many different scientists come to study Antarctica.__
4. If you are a researcher in Antarctica, is there a good chance you will meet other researchers who don't speak your language? How do you know? __Yes; researchers come from about thirty countries.__

Antarctica, with all its beauty, is not an easy place to live. In December and January there are up to 20 hours of sunlight during the month. That means almost total darkness during the winter. That's when the temperature can plunge to -100°F (-38°C)! People who've been here for at least a year can sometimes feel and act like prisoners of war.

Day #3

1. What are the root and the suffix of *darkness*? __root: dark, suffix: -ness__
2. What other word could you use instead of *plunge*? __drop, fall, go down__
3. Which fact about Antarctica from this paragraph do you find the most surprising? __Answers will vary.__
4. What is the most amount of sun in Antarctica during the entire month of December or January? __20 hours in the month__

While the researchers are serious about their work, they have fun, too. In their free time, they play pool and video games and read good books from the station libraries. There are concerts and festivals celebrating the first and last days of sun. Feasts, plays, songs, and games take center court around June 22. What's the reason for all the celebration? Antarctica's winter is half over!

Day #4

1. Does *pool* rhyme with **good book**? __no__
2. What is an antonym for *delicious*? __disgusting, yucky, gross__
3. The author forgot to add this sentence to the passage: "The knowledge they have gained through the research done here has helped the worlds of medicine, science, and conservation." In which paragraph would this sentence best fit? __the paragraph that explains who studies at the research stations__
4. What is happening in North America around June 22? __the beginning of summer__

Assessment

Show Time

(1) This light show lasts about 15 to 40 minutes. It can happen again two or three hours later. The wind on an Antarctic day can whip around at 200 miles an hour (322 km/hr). It's nice to know this phenomenon is around to warm any hearts.

(2) Antarctica's Aurora Australis can be seen almost every night in the winter. Usually, auroras are shaped like curtains hanging in the sky or as streamers or curves of light. The colors range from red to violet but are mostly light green or pink.

(3) Four words are often used to describe Antarctica. They are *dry*, *frigid*, *windy*, and *remote*. Visitors here also have high praise for this icy wonderland, particularly when the Aurora Australis lights up the sky.

(4) An aurora is a burst of energy that appears in the sky. It all starts 50 to 100 miles (80–129 km) above Earth's surface. Protons and electrons are given off by the sun. These particles crash into gases in the Earth's magnetic field. Then, the atoms get electrified. This produces colored light. Because Antarctica is south of the equator, it is in the Southern Hemisphere. Auroras here are called Aurora Australis. Another name is the Southern Lights. Auroras north of the equator are called Aurora Borealis.

1. In which word is the vowel pair *au* pronounced the same as the *o* in the word? __aurora__
2. What does *remote* mean: **far away** or a channel-changing device? __far away__
3. What is the main subject of this article? __the Aurora Australis light show__
4. What is the difference between the Aurora Australis and the Aurora Borealis? __The Aurora Australis takes place in the Southern Hemisphere; the Aurora Borealis, in the Northern Hemisphere.__
5. The article is jumbled. Reread it carefully to figure out which paragraph opens the article, which ones follow, and which one ends it. First comes paragraph __3__, then __4__, then __2__, and then __1__.

Sollie, the Rock

I've lived on a lake for most of my life. I love water sports, especially water skiing. That's why I invited my best friend, Sollie, over to give it a try. Sollie had never been on skis before, but I knew Dad could help him learn.

Day #1

1. What clues does the title give us about the story? __Someone named Sollie will be in it.__
2. Is Sollie an actual rock? __no__
3. Who is Sollie? __the author's best friend__
4. Does the first paragraph tell us what Sollie has to do with a rock? __no__

Water skiing is like flying. I thought it would be easy. Sollie is a seal, sleek and smooth in the water. I thought someone so agile would find skiing easy. It didn't dawn on me until the fourth try that Sollie is more like a rock than a bird.

Day #2

1. Does Sollie quickly learn to water ski? __no__
2. What clues from the paragraph helped you answer #1? __It takes at least four tries.__
3. Predict why Sollie might be more like a rock than a bird when he learns how to water ski. __The author compares Sollie with a rock. A rock sinks, and a bird flies.__
4. Which sentence above uses a metaphor? (for example, Bobby is a mouse) __Sollie is a seal, sleek and smooth in the water.__

On his first try, Sollie let go of the tow rope when Dad hit the gas. He sank like the *Titanic*. On his second try, Sollie leaned into the skis, flipping head over heels like a gymnast falling off the balance beam.

Day #3

1. What is the *Titanic*? __a large ship that sank__
2. Do you know because of knowledge you already have or because you are making an inference? __Answers will vary.__
3. Which sentence in the paragraph uses a simile? (for example, Bobby is *like* a mouse) __He sank like the *Titanic*. Sollie leaned into the skis, flipping head over heels like a gymnast.__
4. How many metaphors are in the paragraph? __two__

On the third try, Sollie stood up. He teetered forward and then back, as if he were a rag doll. He held on to the rope after he lost both skis. He flopped about behind the boat like a giant carp until he finally let go. On the fourth try, Sollie straightened his back and flew around the lake behind the boat as if he were a professional skier.

Day #4

1. Which is your favorite simile in the last paragraph? Why? __Answers will vary.__
2. Make a chart of the different kinds of things the author compares Sollie with. Use these categories: animals, people, things. __Chart should include all the information. One sample is that a person is compared with a seal and a giant carp.__
3. Which category does the author use most often? __things__
4. Look back up to the title. Is the title a metaphor or a simile? __a metaphor__

Assessment

1. Glance down at the selection. What kind of writing is this? __a poem__

Whitesox

Sanding the board,
My cat, Whitesox.

2. What is Whitesox? Why do you think it was given that name? __a cat; because it has white fur on its feet.__

Her tongue,
Like fine grains of sand
On paper,
Licking the wood.

3. What simile is in the above selection? __Her tongue is like fine grains of sand on paper.__

She is an electric sander
Giving out a quiet purr.
Like a nail file,
Smoothing out the edges.

4. When the author compares Whitesox with an electric sander, is that a metaphor or a simile? __a metaphor__
5. Do you think a cat's tongue is rough or smooth? Why? __rough; the metaphor talks about sand, which is grainy__

Answer Key

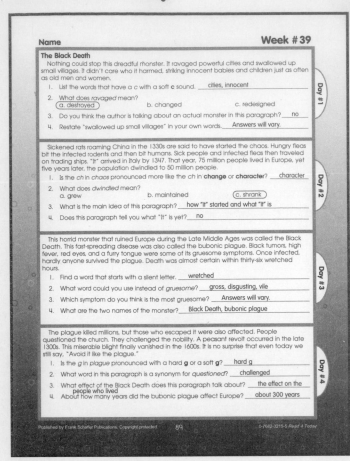

The Black Death

Nothing could stop this dreadful monster. It ravaged powerful cities and swallowed up small villages. It didn't care who it harmed, striking innocent babies and children just as often as old men and women.

Day #1

1. List the words that have a *c* with a soft **c** sound. _____cities, innocent_____

2. What does *ravaged* mean?
   (a. destroyed) b. changed c. redesigned

3. Do you think the author is talking about an actual monster in this paragraph? ___no___

4. Restate "swallowed up small villages" in your own words. ___Answers will vary.___

Sickened rats roaming China in the 1330s are said to have started the chaos. Hungry fleas bit the infected rodents and then bit humans. Sick people and infected fleas then traveled on trading ships. "It" arrived in Italy by 1347. That year, 75 million people lived in Europe, yet five years later, the population dwindled to 50 million people.

Day #2

1. Is the *ch* in *chaos* pronounced more like the *ch* in **change** or **character**? ___character___

2. What does *dwindled* mean?
   a. grew b. maintained (c. shrank)

3. What is the main idea of this paragraph? ___how "It" started and what "It" is___

4. Does this paragraph tell you what "It" is yet? ___no___

This horrid monster that ruined Europe during the Late Middle Ages was called the Black Death. This fast-spreading disease was also called the bubonic plague. Black tumors, high fever, red eyes, and a furry tongue were some of its gruesome symptoms. Once infected, hardly anyone survived the plague. Death was almost certain within thirty-six wretched hours.

Day #3

1. Find a word that starts with a silent letter. ___wretched___

2. What word could you use instead of *gruesome*? ___gross, disgusting, vile___

3. Which symptom do you think is the most gruesome? ___Answers will vary.___

4. What are the two names of the monster? ___Black Death, bubonic plague___

The plague killed millions, but those who escaped it were also affected. People questioned the church. They challenged the nobility. A peasant revolt occurred in the late 1300s. This miserable blight finally vanished in the 1600s. It is no surprise that even today we still say, "Avoid it like the plague."

Day #4

1. Is the *g* in *plague* pronounced with a hard **g** or a soft **g**? ___hard g___

2. What word in this paragraph is a synonym for *questioned*? ___challenged___

3. What effect of the Black Death does this paragraph talk about? ___the effect on the people who lived___

4. About how many years did the bubonic plague affect Europe? ___about 300 years___

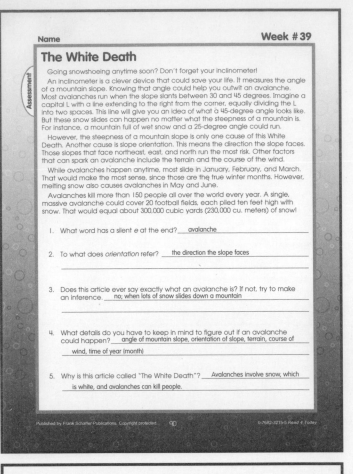

Assessment

The White Death

Going snowshoeing anytime soon? Don't forget your inclinometer!

An inclinometer is a clever device that could save your life. It measures the angle of a mountain slope. Knowing that angle could help you outwit an avalanche. Most avalanches run when the slope slants between 30 and 45 degrees. Imagine a capital L with a line extending to the right from the corner, equally dividing the L into two spaces. This line will give you an idea of what a 45-degree angle looks like. But these snow slides can happen no matter what the steepness of a mountain is. For instance, a mountain full of wet snow and a 25-degree angle could run.

However, the steepness of a mountain slope is only one cause of this White Death. Another cause is slope orientation. This means the direction the slope faces. Those slopes that face northeast, east, and north run the most risk. Other factors that can spark an avalanche include the terrain and the course of the wind.

While avalanches happen anytime, most slide in January, February, and March. That would make the most sense, since those are the true winter months. However, melting snow also causes avalanches in May and June.

Avalanches kill more than 150 people all over the world every year. A single, massive avalanche could cover 20 football fields, each piled ten feet high with snow. That would equal about 300,000 cubic yards (230,000 cu. meters) of snow!

1. What word has a silent *e* at the end? ___avalanche___

2. To what does *orientation* refer? ___the direction the slope faces___
   _____

3. Does this article ever say exactly what an avalanche is? If not, try to make an inference. ___no; when lots of snow slides down a mountain___
   _____

4. What details do you have to keep in mind to figure out if an avalanche could happen? ___angle of mountain slope, orientation of slope, terrain, course of wind, time of year (month)___

5. Why is this article called "The White Death"? ___Avalanches involve snow, which is white, and avalanches can kill people.___

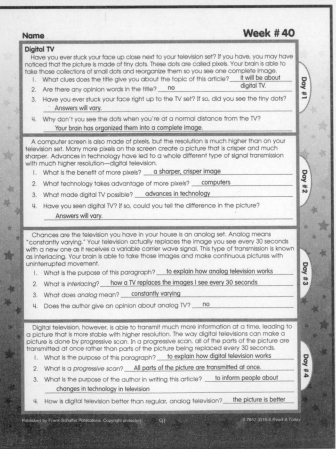

Digital TV

Have you ever stuck your face up close next to your television set? If you have, you may have noticed that the picture is made of tiny dots. These dots are called pixels. Your brain is able to take those collections of small dots and reorganize them so you see one complete image.

Day #1

1. What clues does the title give you about the topic of this article? ___It will be about digital TV.___

2. Are there any opinion words in the title? ___no___

3. Have you ever stuck your face right up to the TV set? If so, did you see the tiny dots? ___Answers will vary.___

4. Why don't you see the dots when you're at a normal distance from the TV? ___Your brain has organized them into a complete image.___

A computer screen is also made of pixels, but the resolution is much higher than on your television set. Many more pixels on the screen create a picture that is crisper and much sharper. Advances in technology have led to a whole different type of signal transmission with much higher resolution—digital television.

Day #2

1. What is the benefit of more pixels? ___a sharper, crisper image___

2. What technology takes advantage of more pixels? ___computers___

3. What made digital TV possible? ___advances in technology___

4. Have you seen digital TV? If so, could you tell the difference in the picture? ___Answers will vary.___

Chances are the television you have in your house is an analog set. Analog means "constantly varying." Your television actually replaces the image you see every 30 seconds with a new one as it receives a variable carrier wave signal. This type of transmission is known as interlacing. Your brain is able to take those images and make continuous pictures with uninterrupted movement.

Day #3

1. What is the purpose of this paragraph? ___to explain how analog television works___

2. What is *interlacing*? ___how a TV replaces the images I see every 30 seconds___

3. What does *analog* mean? ___constantly varying___

4. Does the author give an opinion about analog TV? ___no___

Digital television, however, is able to transmit much more information at a time, leading to a picture that is more stable with higher resolution. The way digital televisions can make a picture is done by progressive scan. In a progressive scan, all of the parts of the picture are transmitted at once rather than the picture being replaced every 30 seconds.

Day #4

1. What is the purpose of this paragraph? ___to explain how digital television works___

2. What is a *progressive scan*? ___All parts of the picture are transmitted at once.___

3. What is the purpose of the author in writing this article? ___to inform people about changes in technology in television___

4. How is digital television better than regular, analog television? ___the picture is better___

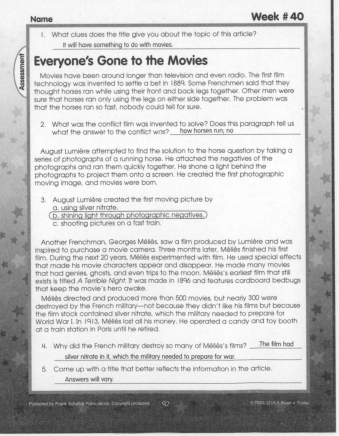

Assessment

1. What clues does the title give you about the topic of this article? ___It will have something to do with movies.___

Everyone's Gone to the Movies

Movies have been around longer than television and even radio. The first film technology was invented to settle a bet in 1889. Some Frenchmen said that they thought horses ran while using their front and back legs together. Other men were sure that horses ran only using the legs on either side together. The problem was that the horses ran so fast, nobody could tell for sure.

2. What was the conflict film was invented to solve? Does this paragraph tell us what the answer to the conflict was? ___how horses run; no___

August Lumière attempted to find the solution to the horse question by taking a series of photographs of a running horse. He attached the negatives of the photographs and ran them quickly together. He shone a light behind the photographs to project them onto a screen. He created the first photographic moving image, and movies were born.

3. August Lumière created the first moving picture by
   a. using silver nitrate.
   (b. shining light through photographic negatives.)
   c. shooting pictures on a fast train.

Another Frenchman, Georges Méliès, saw a film produced by Lumière and was inspired to purchase a movie camera. Three months later, Méliès finished his first film. During the next 20 years, Méliès experimented with film. He used special effects that made his movie characters appear and disappear. He made many movies that had genies, ghosts, and even trips to the moon. Méliès's earliest film that still exists is titled *A Terrible Night*. It was made in 1896 and features cardboard bedbugs that keep the movie's hero awake.

Méliès directed and produced more than 500 movies, but nearly 300 were destroyed by the French military—not because they didn't like his films but because the film stock contained silver nitrate, which the military needed to prepare for World War I. In 1913, Méliès lost all his money. He operated a candy and toy booth at a train station in Paris until he retired.

4. Why did the French military destroy so many of Méliès's films? ___The film had silver nitrate in it, which the military needed to prepare for war.___

5. Come up with a title that better reflects the information in the article. ___Answers will vary.___
